Take a Hint

An A–Z of Money
Time and Labour Savers

Audrey Wilson

CASSELL
LONDON

For Alyce Garfath
who missed the fun of it

CASSELL LTD.
35 Red Lion Square, London WC1R 4SG
and at Sydney, Auckland, Toronto, Johannesburg,
an affiliate of
Macmillan Publishing Co., Inc.,
New York

First published 1979

ISBN 0 304 30228 7

Printed and bound in Great Britain at
The Camelot Press Ltd, Southampton

Contents

Introduction

Take a Hint covers many aspects of family life from early morning (if you are a heavy sleeper, stand the alarm clock on a tin plate) to the end of the day (for tired, aching feet put two tablespoonfuls of paraffin oil into a footbath).

There is advice for young mothers (if baby is restless, switch on the vacuum cleaner to lull him off to sleep) and for fathers (to relieve a hangover, pack a rubber glove with ice cubes and put it on your forehead).

The cook with an underdone cake is advised to cut out the centre and pretend that it was always meant to be a fruit ring. The cake burner should seize a grater, and a ration of rum, and thus she can be handing round chocolate truffles before her guests can say 'King Alfred'.

Child care, cleaning, cooking, decorating, entertaining, gardening, hobbies, house maintenance, invalid care, knitting, laundering, pets and sewing are among the subjects covered in *Take a Hint*. It is not, however, intended to be a set of instructions on homecraft. It aims to supply the frills, assuming a knowledge of the basic rules.

By dipping into these pages, you will find hints, short cuts and bright ideas which would otherwise be acquired only after years of practical experience. Or, if you have no problems, perhaps there will be something to make you reflect, with W. S. Gilbert:

'Oh, don't the days seem lank and long,
 When all goes right and nothing goes wrong!'

Eating
Pancakes to picnics

Kitchen lore abounds with hints for saving money, time and labour but, just as one woman's tedium is another woman's joy, so also one person's life-saver can be an extravagance to another.

Of all the domestic tasks, it is probable that in feeding the family you are offered most scope for saving money if you have time to spare and for saving time if you have money to spare. And the good ideas which cut both corners and costs are the most welcome of all for the mental library of household hints which we all inevitably build up over the years.

I always give full marks to the woman who invests in a pressure cooker. Mine cost about £4 when the weekly food bill for three of us was about £1.50. It seemed an extravagance at the time but, thirty years on, it is my number one friend in the kitchen for saving both time and money.

Getting to know your pressure cooker can bring anxious moments, but don't be discouraged. You will discover that most pressure cooker enthusiasts leapt behind the kitchen door for protection the first time they experienced the violence of the hissing steam, just as you did. But steam pressure is what it is all about, reducing cooking time to a fraction of that required in an ordinary saucepan and, obviously, saving gas and electricity costs.

When a meal is running late, I love the busy hiss of the pressure cooker with its reassurance that food is on the way. The saving in meal preparation time is considerable and, for the working couple in particular, a pressure cooker is invaluable in providing quick meals with little effort.

You can cook a small joint of beef or a piece of ham in less than half an hour and you can buy the cheaper cuts in confident knowledge that they will be quickly cooked to tender perfection. When using up leftovers, I always re-heat cooked meat in the pressure cooker to ensure that a safety level in temperature has been reached.

When soup-making, you can extract every atom of goodness from a marrow bone without the usual long hours of smelly and steamy simmering. The concentrated stock can be frozen and used as required for soups and gravies and the extracted fat can be used for pastry.

Timing instructions for vegetables and fruit must be followed precisely to avoid over-cooking, but you will learn to adapt the size of vegetables to enable several which require differing times to be cooked together.

At some time we all work under pressure in the kitchen, irrespective of the type of cooking equipment we use, and thus it is a natural generator of bright ideas and short cuts whether our interest lies in easier eating or more colourful cooking. When one second saved is important, the useful tip is born.

In such circumstances, I first seized a handy milk bottle to save a few steps to the rolling pin when making pastry and, at that moment, my rolling pin became redundant. It was not to lie useless, however, for it was soon called upon to serve at the church altar when a new paschal candle-holder failed to arrive on time.

We screwed a round tin to one end of the rolling pin and a firm square base to the other. With several coats of gold paint disguising its secular origins, it fulfilled its task of supporting the outsize candle throughout Easter with dignity and without arousing comment.

On another occasion in the kitchen, a friend saw me using a grater to make breadcrumbs.

'That's a good idea,' she said.

'Is there any other way?' I reacted.

Until then she had just crumbled bread between her fingers to reduce it to breadcrumbs.

Now she uses a grater and I'm a finger-crumbler.

Almonds Blanch almonds by immersing them in boiling water for a few minutes, then plunge them into cold water and you will find that the skins rub off easily. You can moisten dry almonds by soaking them in milk before use.

For an economical almond paste, mix some semolina and almond essence with the ground almonds.

Apples will not discolour after peeling if you keep them in salted water until needed.

In pies and charlottes, apples will cook more quickly if you grate them.

When baking apples, split the skin half-way down to save baking time. For a pleasant variation, stuff apples with mincemeat or with a sage and onion mixture to serve with pork.

You can vary the flavour of an apple pie by adding mixed spice instead of cloves, by adding grated cheese to the pastry mixture or by topping the apples with cinnamon and brown sugar on buttered bread.

Store apples in a stocking after smearing them with petroleum jelly to prevent wrinkling, tie a knot between each one and hang them up. Peel them before use. Surplus apples will take up less storage space if they are pulped and bottled or frozen in plastic tubs.

Turn windfalls into apple jelly; it is not necessary to peel or core them. Make mint jelly by adding chopped mint to some of the apple jelly as it reaches setting point.

You can add fine breadcrumbs to apple sauce to increase the quantity and, if you have to use eating apples for making a sauce, add lemon juice to sharpen the flavour.

Asparagus Open a tin of asparagus at the bottom to keep the tips whole.

Baby foods will heat up economically in an egg poacher.

Tins of sweet and savoury baby foods can be used as sauces and vol-au-vent fillings.

Bacon To save time and to have bacon rashers ready for immediate use in the morning, trim all the rinds and snip the edges before you store them away.

Soak salty bacon in hot water to remove the excess salt and soak dry bacon in milk or water to soften it before frying.

For crisp bacon, stretch the rasher with a knife before grilling or frying it. A dusting of flour will reduce shrinkage and snipping the edges of a rasher will prevent curling.

Make a stock for soups and gravies by simmering bacon rinds in water. Keep it in the fridge, or freeze it, for use as required.

Baked beans   Use a porringer or double saucepan for heating baked beans to make the cleaning of the pan easier.

Bananas   Slice bananas into lemon juice to prevent discoloration.

You can make a quick cream by whisking together a mashed banana and the white of an egg.

Basting   A muslin bag filled with suet and herbs tied to the oven bars above a roast will baste the joint without effort.

Batter   Vary the flavour of a coating batter by adding dried onions and herbs to it.

Bazaars   When sending contributions for a cake stall, line the pie dish or cake tin with aluminium foil before baking, so that you will have a ready-made protective non-returnable packing for your gift.

Beetroot   Reduce bleeding when cooking beetroot by twisting off the stalks instead of cutting them off.

To peel beetroot, put the hot cooked beetroot into cold water. The skin will rub off easily with your fingers.

Cooked beetroot can be chopped with an egg-slicer and it can also be grated for easy handling in sandwiches.

Make beetroot jelly by chopping the beetroot into small pieces and adding a packet of lemon jelly to hot vinegar. Preserve it in a screwtop jar or, for a longer period, in a plastic tub in the freezer.

Birthday cakes   A sponge cake cut into varied chunky shapes and covered with fudge icing makes a realistic moon-landing setting. Complete the scene with a space-ship bearing a 'Happy Birthday' pennant and some astronauts, one for each child.

Green icing will convert an oval cake into a racing track with miniature cars set around the course.

Put a swiss roll on a rectangular piece of cake as the base for a railway engine. Cut out suitable shapes of cake for the cab, dome and funnel and stick them in place with icing. Cover the engine with chocolate icing and add appropriate detail with piped white icing. Dark chocolate vermicelli makes realistic coal for a tank engine. Make the wheels from small ginger biscuits with icing 'spokes'.

Chocolate drops can be used as roof tiles on a cottage cake and mints with a hole in the middle make port-holes for ships.

Instead of a large cake, make small cakes in baking cases and pipe one letter of HAPPY BIRTHDAY on each cake.

Biscuits   Keep a lump of sugar in the biscuit tin or line it with blotting-paper to keep the biscuits fresh.

When biscuit crumbs are required for a recipe, put the biscuits into a paper bag and crush them with a rolling pin.

For emergency fancy biscuits, sandwich plain biscuits with butter icing or put a chocolate drop or half a marshmallow on them and put them briefly under a hot grill.

To open a packet of Cellophane-wrapped biscuits quickly, cut it in half with a sharp knife.

For made-in-a-moment no-baking biscuits, dissolve 4 oz (113 g) margarine, 4 oz toffee and 4 oz marshmallows in a large saucepan. Stir into the mixture a small packet of grain-type breakfast cereal. Spread it in a greased tin and leave until cold.

When making biscuits, to save time cutting them out form the mixture into a long roll and cut it into thin slices.

Blancmange   Give blancmange a creamier flavour by adding a large knob of butter and prevent skin forming by covering the mould with greaseproof paper, aluminium foil or plastic film.

Boiling economy   Use a large saucepan when boiling puddings and cook potatoes and other vegetables in it at the same time.

Any saucepan can be converted to a double saucepan with a pudding cloth. Place the vegetables on the cloth and knot the four corners on the outside of the lid so that the vegetables are suspended below the lid.

Food such as potatoes, rice, stews, porridge and fruit put into a vacuum flask at boiling point will continue to cook for many hours.

Brandy snaps   To achieve the speed necessary to cope with a freshly-baked tray of brandy snaps, keep half-a-dozen short lengths of dowelling handy and use them successively for rolling the biscuits.

Brandy snaps can also be shaped into cones and filled with chopped pineapple and cream.

Bread   Place a wire cake tray at the bottom of the bread tin to keep the bread crisp longer.

Fresh bread will be easier to cut if you dip the knife into hot water. To make bread easier to grate first break it into pieces and sprinkle them with flour.

Brush a stale loaf with water or milk and put it into a moderately hot oven to allow it to dry out and regain its freshness.

When re-heating bread rolls, put them inside a wet paper bag in a hot oven for five minutes.

Surplus bread and butter will keep fresh if you wrap it in aluminium foil.

Sprinkle stale bread and butter with salt, or soak it in beaten egg, and fry it to use as a base for savouries.

Breadcrumbs   Bake stale bread slowly in the oven until it is brown and crisp, then crush it inside a paper bag to make coating crumbs for frying. Store it in a screwtop jar.

When a recipe requires breadcrumbs, save time by soaking the stated amount of crustless bread in the wet ingredients and mashing it with a fork, instead of making breadcrumbs in the usual way.

Crushed cornflakes substitute very well for breadcrumbs in treacle tarts and for coating fish.

Bread snacks   Turn crusts and stale bread into cheese snacks by coating them with butter and grated cheese and baking them until brown and crisp.

Brown sugar which has hardened will soften if left in a basin covered with a damp cloth.

Butter   Creaming butter and sugar is easier if the sugar and the mixing bowl are warmed before use or if you grate the butter into the bowl on a warmed grater. Some types of potato masher make quick work of blending butter and sugar.

Hard butter can be softened by putting a hot basin over the butter dish, by holding the unwrapped packet under the hot tap for a few seconds, by mixing in a few drops of boiling water with the butter or by warming it with a hairdryer.

Make butter pats quickly from hard butter with an apple corer either by 'peeling' it or 'coring' it.

Cabbage   Counteract the smell of boiling cabbage by putting a piece of celery, parsley or a squeeze of lemon juice in the saucepan or a slice of bread on top of the cabbage.

If you have only large cabbages in the garden when you need a small amount, cut off sufficient for the meal and leave the remainder growing until required.

Cakes   Protect a slowly-cooking rich fruit cake from burning by wrapping several thicknesses of brown paper around the cake tin.

Cover a cake in its final stages of baking with a butter wrapper or aluminium foil to prevent it from burning.

When testing to see if a cake is cooked, always heat the knife or knitting needle first.

A cake with a sunken centre can be served hot as a pudding and the hollow filled with warmed jam or fruit. Soggy cake can also be turned into biscuits by adding more flour, rolling it out and re-baking.

If a cake is likely to crumble at the centre when you slice it, dip a round pastry cutter in hot water and press it through the middle of the cake, then cut each slice up to the centre circle so that a thin crumbling end is avoided.

An oven-glass jelly mould will produce an attractively-shaped cake.

Syrup, marmalade or crushed pineapple will help to make a rich fruit cake moist; other liquid ingredients should be reduced accordingly.

To ensure a flat top for a rich fruit cake, make a hollow in the centre of the cake mixture before you put it in the oven.

Fruit cake will stay moist for a long time if a sliced eating apple is placed in the tin. The texture of a dry cake can be improved with this treatment.

You can prevent cream from oozing out when you slice a sponge cake by cutting the top half into slices before placing it on the cream.

When filling paper cases with cake mixture, use a teaspoon in each hand or dip the spoon into milk between each filling to prevent the mixture from sticking and falling unevenly.

When beating up a cake mixture, steady the bowl on a damp cloth.

A mixture of rolled oats and sugar sprinkled on a cake before cooking produces a crisp topping.

The burnt part of a cake can be carefully grated off.

If a hot cake will not leave its tin, stand it in cold water; if a cooled-off cake refuses to move, stand the tin in hot water. In both cases, run a knife around the sides of the tin in gentle persuasion.

To prevent new tins sticking, grease them well and bake them empty in the oven before bringing them into use.

Greasing is easier if you warm the tins first.

Cake candles Chill candles overnight in the freezer to make them burn evenly without dripping.

Sweets, especially those with a hole in the middle, and large poppet beads make attractive candle-holders.

Cake decoration Animal-shaped biscuit cutters will give you an outline to ice on a cake.

Tie a band of greaseproof paper or aluminium foil around a cake to obtain a straight edge when icing the top only.

Use sterilized eyebrow tweezers to place small decorations on a cake; use a cocktail stick, dipped in colouring, to write on white icing; use a skewer when coating madeleines with jam and coconut; use a potato peeler on a slab of chocolate to make a quick topping.

Place a paper doyley on top of a sponge and sieve icing sugar over it. Remove the doyley carefully to reveal a lacy decoration.

For instant icing, grate chocolate on cakes as soon as you take them out of the oven.

A decorated cake will be easier to handle if you store it on the lid of the tin and place the bottom section over it.

Put a strip of greaseproof paper or aluminium foil around a cake before fixing the frill so that you can preserve the latter for re-use.

Carrots Add a knob of butter or dripping when boiling carrots to improve the flavour and to lessen the risk of their burning.

Cheese Keep cheese fresh and free from mould by wrapping it in polythene or in a cloth soaked in vinegar. A sugar cube in the cheese dish keeps it fresh.

If you often use cheese for soups and sauces save time by grating a whole pound of cheese at a time and storing it in an air-tight container in the fridge.

Use a potato peeler to grate cheese when only a small quantity is needed; it is easier to clean than a grater.

Chestnuts can be roasted without burning your fingers if you put them in a wire chip-basket. If you have no open fire, boil the chestnuts and then grill them for a crisp finish.

Chips will brown more quickly if you add a pinch of salt to the fat and they will be crisper if you prick them with a fork before frying.

Chips can be partly cooked in boiling water some hours before they are needed and dried so that they are ready for speedy frying at the meal-time.

Chocolate A bar of chocolate grated into a little hot milk or evaporated milk makes a quick sauce.

Use coffee or orange juice to vary the flavour of chocolate icings and instant dessert powders.

Coconut For cake decoration, brown desiccated coconut under a low grill, turning it over as it darkens. It can also be coloured by shaking it up with some colouring essence.

Coffee A pinch of salt added to the grounds improves the flavour of coffee.

After making coffee by the jug method, add a few drops of cold water to make the grounds settle at the bottom.

Grind fresh coffee grounds to a very fine powder to make your own instant coffee.

Fill a jar with a mixture of one part of instant coffee powder to three parts of dried milk powder and make creamy coffee by mixing the required amount to a paste with cold water in a cup. Then pour on boiling water.

Cookery books can be protected from splashes when you are following a recipe by putting them, opened at the correct page, inside a plastic bag.

If you have a drop-down door to a kitchen cupboard, it will make an ideal holder for your cookery book. Fit a length of wood to support the book with two wooden or metal clips to hold the pages open.

Corks To ensure easy withdrawal of a cork, when you insert it put a strip of tape across the bottle opening and push it in with the cork, leaving the ends exposed.

A cloth soaked in very hot water and wrapped around the neck of a bottle will loosen a tight cork.

If a cork is slightly too large for a bottle, you can make it fit by cutting out a thin wedge across its diameter.

To extract a cork which has dropped inside a bottle, thread a button on to the middle of a strong thread and, holding the ends, put the button into the bottle and use it to manoeuvre the cork through the neck of the bottle.

A crochet hook is useful for extracting a cork which has broken in the neck of a bottle.

Cottage pie will be crisper if you put a layer of breadcrumbs between the meat and the potatoes.

Cream To empty a bottle completely of thick cream, hold it under a hot tap.

Add the whisked white of an egg when whipping full cream to make a lighter cream and a greater quantity.

Cucumber sandwiches are easier to handle if the cucumber is grated instead of sliced.

For cocktail snacks, cut a cucumber in half lengthways then chop it into small pieces, scoop out the centres and fill them with salmon or chopped ham.

Cupful To measure half a cupful of fat, half fill a cup with cold water and drop in sufficient fat to raise the water to the top of the cup. The amount of fat used is half a cupful.

Currants Keep your hands clean when picking black or red currants by using a large table fork to pull the currants off their stems.

Custard tarts To ensure that the pastry stays at the bottom of the dish, press out all the air between the pastry and the bottom and sides of the dish. Partly bake the case empty, with a layer of dried beans or a slightly smaller tin weighing it down. Have the hot milk and egg mixture standing ready in a pan of hot water and pour it on the pastry to complete its cooking time.

Dates are easily chopped up with a heated knife.

Dried fruit such as prunes and figs can be left overnight in a vacuum flask of boiling water to be ready to eat in the morning.

Save time by washing and drying dried fruit for cakes as soon as you buy it, then keep it in a screwtop jar so that small quantities will be readily available when needed.

To get rid of stones after washing and rinsing sultanas and raisins, drop the fruit, a few at a time, on a baking tin. The sound of any stones dropping can be easily heard and the interlopers removed.

A hairdryer will dry fruit quickly.

Dried fruit soaked overnight in cold tea will make cakes and scones moist.

Eggs An egg-white will stiffen more quickly if you add a pinch of salt. When beating whites and yolks separately, always beat the whites first to keep them free of any yolk left on the whisk as this would prevent them from stiffening.

Prevent a cracked egg from deteriorating by sealing the crack with Sellotape or by dipping it in boiling water for a few seconds.

When a cracked egg sticks to the cardboard carton, soak it in cold water to free it.

Add salt or vinegar to the water when boiling a cracked egg to keep it intact.

Prick a small hole in the pointed end of an egg to prevent it from bursting while boiling.

An insufficiently-boiled egg can be returned to the pan wrapped in aluminium foil to continue cooking.

Put hard-boiled eggs into cold water as soon as they are cooked and tap them all over on a hard surface to make them peel easily.

To mash up boiled eggs quickly for sandwiches, use a grater or put the egg through a slicer twice, lengthways and widthways.

If you use an ordinary saucepan for poaching eggs, grease it with butter or olive oil to prevent the eggs from sticking to one another or to the pan bottom. The whites will solidify quickly if you add vinegar to the water.

An egg can be poached conveniently in an oiled soup ladle or in an aluminium foil baking case.

You can use a fancy biscuit cutter to poach or fry eggs to appeal to children.

A dozen eggs can be poached at a time by using a patty tin inside a roasting tin filled with hot water.

Avoid difficult saucepan cleaning by cooking scrambled eggs in a greased basin standing in a pan of boiling water.

Half a teaspoonful of cornflour added to a scrambled egg mixture ensures a good texture. Breadcrumbs can be added to increase the quantity.

Separate the white from the yolk by breaking an egg into a funnel or tea strainer, or by holding an egg-cup over the yolk on a saucer and pouring off the white, or by lifting out the yolk slowly with a dessertspoon.

Yolks of egg will keep in the refrigerator without hardening if covered in water until needed. Left-over whisked egg can be frozen and stored.

Poach spare egg yolks and mix with grated cheese to make a sandwich spread. Add salad cream or mayonnaise for extra tang, if desired, and to avoid dryness.

Children who dislike eggs will absorb the yolk happily if it is beaten into mashed potato, tomato soup or baked beans.

Cover a cup of egg-white with aluminium foil to keep it fresh until needed.

Use spare egg-whites to make meringues and macaroons, to glaze pastry, dredging it with sugar, or add it to ground rice puddings and custards.

Egg substitutes   Custard powder and milk can be used to coat fish with breadcrumbs for frying.

When mixing a cake, if you find the egg-yolks are pale add some custard powder for a better colour and reduce the amount of flour used accordingly.

Where several eggs are recommended for a cake, one tablespoonful of vinegar can be substituted for one of the eggs.

Evaporated milk will whisk up to a thick cream if the tin is boiled for five minutes and left overnight to cool.

Feeding   Stand your baby's high chair on a large plastic tablecloth at meal-times to protect the floor from spills.

A slippery high-chair seat can be made safer by sticking a sheet of plastic foam to it.

Fish will be easier to grip when filleting if you dip your fingers in salt first. You will find sterilized eyebrow tweezers useful for removing the bones.

If you have no fridge, you can keep fish fresh overnight in warm weather by covering it with greaseproof paper well sprinkled with salt.

Tie a piece of white cotton around cod steaks to keep them whole or to hold a savoury stuffing in place.

Soft roes are easier to handle if you scald them first with boiling water for a few minutes before flouring them.

For a change, when frying fish coat it with sage and onion stuffing mixture or with the mixture added to the batter.

If you add vinegar to batter it will be extra crisp.

Lemon juice or vinegar will prevent boiled fish from flaking during cooking.

Fish can be easily steamed by placing it on a covered buttered plate or dish over a saucepan of boiling water.

For tastier fish cakes, boil the potatoes in the water in which you have cooked the fish.

To rid a frying pan of a fishy smell, boil some vinegar in it.

Flavouring   A fountain pen filler, a medicine dropper, the tip of a needle or a skewer can all be used to measure drops of flavouring essences. Make sure that these instruments are sterilized first though.

Flouring   To avoid making a mess when flouring, put the flour and seasoning into a paper bag and drop the pieces of fish or meat into it. Afterwards you can throw away the bag.

Food storage   The insulation of an electric oven keeps food cool in hot weather.

Freezers   Write a large number on every package you put in the freezer and keep a running list of the contents. It will be easy to identify the item when needed and to cross it off the list.

Bread keeps well in a freezer and, apart from the convenience of having it in stock, it is a cheap way of keeping the freezer full and thus running economically when other stocks are getting low. Similarly, and cheaper still, empty spaces can be filled with ice cubes stored in plastic bags or with larger blocks of ice made in margarine tubs.

To avoid having to defrost a full packet of sausages when you need only one serving, separate them into single portions before freezing. Other items such as bread, cake, meat and pastes can be treated similarly by the single person.

A nail-brush helps with the quick dispersal of melting frost from the shelves when de-frosting.

Funnels   You can make funnels for filling various sizes of containers from the corners of envelopes, by shaping one from aluminium foil, by making a hole in an empty egg-shell or by using the top of a plastic bottle cut off at the base of the neck.

Gas saving   Make full use of the residual heat in burners and pans when using a gas cooker. Turn off the grill when toasting as soon as the second side starts to colour and let the bread brown in the remaining heat. An egg put into a hot frying pan, and covered with a lid will cook slowly without further gas.

Glacé cherries will not sink to the bottom of the cake if, after washing and drying them, you roll them in flour before adding them to the mixture.

Grapefruit will peel easily if you boil them for a few minutes and then put them into cold water.

Fill empty grapefruit halves with jelly for children's parties.

Dry grapefruit can be made juicy by leaving them for a few hours sprinkled with sugar and a teaspoonful of water.

Grapes   A sterilized hairpin makes easy work of de-pipping grapes.

Gravy   Add sage and onion stuffing or forcemeat mixture to the gravy to add flavour to a meat or sausage dish.

Greaseproof paper   Save butter and other fat wrappers for lining cake tins and for protecting food in the oven from over-browning.

Hot liquids   To prevent fine china or glassware from cracking when hot liquid is poured into it, put a metal teaspoon in first.

Ice cream   Use a hot spoon to serve ice cream straight from the freezer.

Ice cubes   Prevent ice cube trays from sticking to the freezer compartment by lining the shelf with aluminium foil or waxed paper, or by greasing the bottom of the tray with Vaseline.
    Ice cubes made with fruit juice are colourful for a children's party and small fruits, such as cherries and raspberries, can be sealed inside. Chocolate box trays make interesting ice shapes.

Icing   When icing small cakes, save time by dipping the cakes into the icing.
    If you do not possess a revolving icing table, use an upturned cake tin.
    Shape greaseproof paper into a cone for an emergency forcing bag, or use a strong plastic bag with one corner cut off.
    The top of a salt cellar dropped into a forcing bag will substitute for a fine icing cone.
    Use jam or melted jelly cubes to mix and colour icing. Tea will colour icing cream.
    For a glossy chocolate icing, add a knob of butter.
    Coconut will thicken and flavour icing.
    Add a little glycerine to royal icing if you do not want it to set hard.
    Keep a tea infuser in the icing sugar box for quick sprinklings on cakes and pies.
    Pipe surplus icing into flower shapes for cake and dessert decoration.

Jam   A few drops of water sprinkled over the jam will keep jam tarts moist as they cook. Use a grapefruit knife to lift out the cooked tarts.
    Clear the sugariness from stored jam by bringing it to boiling point in a saucepan.
    Smear the bottom and sides of a preserving pan with butter to guard against burning.
    A knob of butter in the preserving pan gives the jam a brighter appearance and makes the scum easier to remove.
    If jam is not setting, add one tablespoonful of lemon juice to each pound of fruit.

One teaspoonful of glycerine stirred into four pounds of jam just before setting point is reached will help to preserve it.

Jelly   To make a jelly set quickly, dissolve the jelly in a small amount of water and use ice cubes to make up the full quantity of water required.

Kippers   To avoid a strong smell, cook kippers in the oven wrapped in aluminium foil or place them in a covered pan of boiling water for ten minutes.

When grilling kippers, put some hot water in the pan. This will create steam and keep the kippers moist.

Labels for dry food stored in jars will last longer if they are stuck to the inside of the jar.

Lemons   A lemon will yield more juice if you soak it in boiling water before squeezing it.

Prick a lemon with a fork or knitting needle when you need only a few drops.

To remove all the lemon rind from a grater, brush it off with a pastry brush. If you are using a recipe which requires breadcrumbs also, grate the bread after the lemon.

Extract the maximum benefit from lemons by covering the squeezed skins with sugar and boiling water and leaving it overnight to produce a lemon drink. Oranges can be treated in the same way.

Slices of lemon can be frozen individually, then stored in a plastic bag in the freezer.

Lettuces will keep fresh for several days in a saucepan with a tight lid or they can be wrapped in newspaper and kept in a cool place.

Margarine   When opening a packet of margarine, mark it off into sections to obviate the need for weighing it for a recipe.

To extract soft margarine from its tub quickly, stand the tub in hot water for a few seconds.

Mayonnaise   When mixing mayonnaise, have the oil and eggs at room temperature and use a metal spoon for easier mixing.

Milk   To prevent milk from boiling over, stand a pie funnel in the saucepan.

Do not allow milk for coffee to reach boiling point and stir it occasionally to prevent a skin forming.

Rinse a milk saucepan with cold water before use and stand it upside down as soon as you empty it for easy cleaning.

A vacuum flask, rinsed out in cold water beforehand, will keep milk cool.

If you have no fridge a bottle of milk will stay fresh longer if it is covered with a wet cloth, the ends of which are left trailing in water. It is a good idea to make a plastic foam cover for this purpose.

Encourage children to drink milk by whisking one tablespoonful of red jam, a dissolved jelly cube or milk-shake mix into a glass of milk.

Use sour milk to make scones and cakes lighter, or strain it through muslin and season the curds with salt and pepper to make a tasty cottage cheese.

To make Yorkshire curd tart, add 1 oz (28 g) sugar, 1 oz butter, 1 oz currants, 1 egg and grated nutmeg to the curds from one pint of sour milk and fill a pastry case with the mixture. Bake it in a hot oven for about twenty minutes.

Milk pudding Bring a milk pudding mixture to the boil and put it into a heated vacuum flask to continue cooking overnight or throughout the day.

Dolly mixtures scattered on a milk pudding may tempt the reluctant eater.

Minced beef Separate mince from its wrapping paper by holding it under cold water briefly.

Add rolled oats, lentils or a soya preparation to minced beef to make it go further.

Mince Pies Press down mince-pie lids with an egg-cup and make a hole to allow the steam to escape, for a crisper pastry.

As a variation, prise off the lids of mince pies and top them with ice cream, or use meringue topping instead of the pastry lid.

Mincer Clean a mincer after use by passing a piece of stale bread through it.

Bread helps fatty foods to pass through a mincer more easily.

Mint is easier to chop if you sprinkle it with sugar. Mint sauce can be made with lemon juice instead of vinegar, for a change.

For a ready supply of chopped mint throughout the winter, fill ice cube trays with chopped mint. When frozen, put the mint cubes into a plastic bag and store them in the freezer.

Mint leaves can be frozen whole in a plastic bag in the freezer and crushed with a rolling pin when needed.

Mint can be preserved in golden syrup in a screwtop jar. For easy mixing, put a thick layer of chopped mint in the jar followed by one teaspoonful of syrup and continue in this way until the jar is full. Add vinegar to the required amount to make mint sauce.

Newspapers Use newspaper in the kitchen to clean out frying pans, to wrap up all waste for the dustbin, to wrap up lettuces and greens to keep them fresh and to place in front of the cooker to catch splashes when frying.

Night drinks   Use a vacuum flask to keep milk and other drinks hot at the bedside for night-time or early morning requirements.

Nuts which are difficult to crack should be dropped into boiling water for a few minutes and then into cold water.

Those who enjoy nuts but find them difficult to chew can still enjoy the flavour by reducing them to a powder in an electric grinder.

Onions   Make crisp fried onions by dipping the rings into egg-white or evaporated milk and coating them with flour before you fry them. To prevent tears peel an onion downwards to the root or under a running tap.

To take away the smell, chew a mint after eating onions.

Crushed dried onions can be used as a coating for frying.

If you dislike a strong onion flavour in boiled onions, drain off the water when it comes to the boil and start again with fresh water. A piece of bread placed on top of the onions will also reduce the smell.

Oven shelf   A large deep upturned cake-tin placed at the bottom of the oven will serve as an extra shelf.

Pancakes   If you make pancake batter in a jug, you will find it easy to pour the required amount into the frying pan.

Cover cooked pancakes with a colander to keep them hot without losing their crispness.

Parsley   Squeeze parsley tightly after washing it and cut it thinly with scissors to speed up the chopping process.

Make ice cubes of chopped parsley and store them in the freezer, or freeze the parsley whole and crush it when frozen.

Pastry   When making pastry, any surplus can be rolled out and stored in the fridge, or baked 'blind' to use later for a quick flan or fruit tart. A layer of beans will keep the base flat as it bakes or, better still, bake the case on the outside of a tin.

When using a packet of frozen puff pastry for sausage rolls, cut it into a suitable number of pieces and roll each one to sausage roll size.

An excellent way to bake a dozen small cases of short pastry for filling with fruit and cream is on an upturned patty tin.

It is a good idea to use double quantities when rubbing fat into flour for a pastry mix and store the surplus in a plastic bag in the fridge. For quick needs, the mix can be the basis of meat and fruit pies or crumbles, scones or cakes.

If your fat is cold and hard, save time by grating it into the bowl.

Pinking shears make strips of pastry attractive for open tarts.

Sprinkle the mixing bowl with salt after making bread or pastry so that you can rub away the dough remnants easily.

A roll of pastry will make a central support for a pie crust and it will also act as a funnel if you make slits on both sides of it in the centre of the crust. An earthenware stemmed egg-cup or a salt cellar with a hole in its base will also substitute for a pie funnel.

Make a pie easier to serve by marking the top into portions before baking it.

When mixing pastry, keep a plastic bag handy to cover your hand and avoid scattering flour if you have to answer the telephone or find something in a cupboard.

Pears will skin easily if you scald them in boiling water for a few minutes and then put them into cold water. Cover them with salted water after peeling to prevent discoloration if they are not to be eaten immediately.

When bottling pears, scoop out the cores with a teaspoon.

Pickled onions Make a salad dressing from the vinegar in which onions have been bottled by shaking it up with an equal quantity of salad oil. It will also give sliced tomatoes or beetroot a pleasant flavour.

Picnics Picnic food is easier to handle and to protect from flies and other insects if it is packed individually into plastic boxes or empty margarine tubs.

Pork To make crisp crackling when roasting pork, rub salt and olive oil into the scored skin and, for extra crispness, detach it from the joint in the later stages of cooking. Paste a mixture of brown sugar and cider on the skin for a tasty variation.

Dip pork chops into beaten egg and sage and onion stuffing mixture before cooking.

As a change from apple sauce, heat pineapple rings in the pork juices for half an hour before serving.

Potatoes Use a nylon scourer to scrape new potatoes, soaking them first in hot water to loosen the skin.

Old potatoes have a higher vitamin value if they are scraped instead of peeled.

Potatoes peeled in advance will not discolour if you add salt or milk to the water in which they are standing.

Skins of potatoes boiled in their jackets will be easier to remove if they are scored before cooking.

Baked jacket potatoes will cook more quickly if they are boiled for five minutes beforehand or, to save fuel, left standing in hot water for half an hour.

A clean metal skewer pushed through the centre of a large potato will lessen baking time.

For crisp roast potatoes, parboil them and sprinkle them with flour before putting them into the roasting tin.

Potatoes can be baked without fat in an inch of water in a roasting tin.

Remove the centre of a large potato with an apple corer for quicker cooking. The potato could be stuffed with rolled bacon or cheese when it is nearly cooked.

Make potato shells to fill with hot savouries by halving large peeled potatoes, scooping out the centre and frying the shell in deep fat.

To make potato fritters, parboil thick-sliced potatoes, then coat them with batter and fry in deep fat.

Over-cooked potatoes for mashing can be salvaged by sprinkling powdered milk over them.

Save aluminium foil soup packets for baking potatoes on an open fire.

Powders   It is easier and quicker to mix powders such as gravy, custard and instant desserts with a fork rather than a spoon.

Preserving jars   Commercial jam jars and their lids can be used for preserving provided they are tarnish-free with the plastic ring intact. Heat the jars in the oven and boil the lids in a saucepan, pressing them on firmly as soon as you have filled the jars with the hot fruit.

To loosen tight rings on bottling jars, apply a cloth wrung out in hot water.

Prunes   Soak prunes overnight in cold tea for an improved flavour or put them into a heated vacuum flask in strained hot tea so that they will cook without fuel. Brown sugar and lemon juice also improve the flavour of prunes.

Puddings   Save handle-less cups for making individual steamed puddings, jellies and mousses.

Use syrup instead of fat to grease a pudding basin for easy removal of the contents.

When boiling puddings, several large metal lids will substitute for a trivet and protect the basin if the saucepan boils dry. A pebble placed in the saucepan will draw your attention to the need for more water.

Make a pudding basin holder from webbing to ease its safe removal from a hot saucepan. Form a cross with two lengths of webbing, stitching them firmly together at the centre square. Stand the basin on this square and secure the straps with a safety-pin.

Always put a pleat in a pudding basin cloth to allow the mixture to rise.

Radishes After topping and tailing radishes, rub them together between your palms under running water to clean them.

To make decorative radishes, score the skins half-way down about six times and put the radishes into cold water until they open out.

Recipes Paste colourful recipes inside a kitchen cupboard door for inspiration as well as decoration.

When making unusual cakes or biscuits for a bazaar stall, make extra money by selling copies of the recipe.

Revolving tray Screw a round metal tin to a cupboard shelf, with a metal washer in between, to hold spices and other small items.

Rhubarb Add a few red jelly cubes to stewed rhubarb to give it more body and a good colour or add a teaspoonful of sago to thicken the juice as it cooks.

Rice A teaspoonful of lemon juice and a knob of butter will help to keep rice white and fluffy, and a little salad oil will keep the grains separated.

Smear the rim of the saucepan with butter to prevent rice from boiling over.

Use the water in which rice has been boiled for soups and gravies.

For fluffy rice, soak long-grained rice in cold water for 10 minutes before boiling.

Rusks can be made by slicing crustless bread into thick pieces and baking them in a very cool oven.

Salad bowl Place an upturned glass fruit dish or a flower holder inside a salad bowl and build the salad on top of it to allow the moisture to drain to the bottom of the bowl.

Salt Put dried peas, grains of rice or a piece of blotting paper inside a salt cellar to absorb any dampness.

Sandwiches Save time when packing lunches by making a week's supply at a time. Wrapped individually in plastic film or aluminium foil, you can store them in the freezer and dispense them daily.

Lemon juice blended with butter keeps sandwiches moist.

Prevent tomato sandwiches from becoming soggy by grating cheese over them.

Saucepans A saucepan which has lost its handle can be used as a cake tin.

Clamp a spring clothes peg to a mixing spoon to hold it steady on the edge of a saucepan.

Sauces Stop skin forming on a newly-made sauce by covering it with greaseproof paper, plastic film or, in the case of a sweet sauce, a sprinkling of sugar.

Store packet sauces and soups in a toast-rack.

Surplus sauce can be frozen and stored. It is a good idea to make a double quantity with this in mind.

Rinse out empty sauce and pickle bottles with vinegar or warm water before discarding them and add the liquid to soups or stews.

Sausages Cooking sausages on a metal skewer or a steel knitting needle saves time when turning them over.

Instead of separating sausages, unlink them before pricking them and cook them in one piece to retain moisture and avoid hard end pieces.

Dip sausages in beaten egg and roll them in flour, oats or forcemeat mixture for extra crispness and flavour.

Sausages soaked in cold water will skin easily.

If you pour boiling water over sausages after pricking them, they are less likely to burst in cooking.

Scones To have scones which are ready for buttering when cooked without being cut in half, roll the scone mixture to half the usual thickness. Cut out the rounds and cook them in pairs, one on top of the other.

Add grated apple to a scone mixture for a change of flavour.

For moist scones, soak the dried fruit overnight or pour boiling water over it just before use.

For extra lightness, use sour milk or yoghurt when mixing scones.

Scotch eggs For even cooking, wrap Scotch eggs in aluminium foil or place them between two foil baking cases and bake them in the oven.

Scotch pancakes Add a little syrup to a Scotch pancake batter for an improved texture.

Screwtop jars A rubber glove will give you a grip on a difficult lid. A damp towel is also helpful.

Dipping a tight lid into boiling water will often loosen it.

Smells Dispel cooking smells by burning some lavender or by boiling ground cloves or coffee.

A bowl of vinegar placed inside the fridge will remove a strong smell.

Soups A raw potato added to over-salted soup may remove enough of the salt to make the soup palatable.

If soup is left overnight after making, the flavour will improve and any fat will set so that it can be skimmed off easily.

To remove fat from hot soup, wrap an ice cube in tissue paper and run it over the surface of the soup.

Instead of thickening soup with flour or cereals, it can be left to simmer and thicken naturally by evaporation.

Left-over soup can be frozen and stored in plastic bags.

Make two vegetable soups at once by straining off most of the liquid for a clear soup and thickening the remainder with the sieved vegetables.

An egg poached in tomato soup and sprinkled with grated cheese makes a nourishing meal.

Spices   Store spices in unused salt and pepper pots, suitably labelled, or make a set of spice jars from baby food jars.

Steam   Place a terry towel over the plate rack to absorb the steam from boiling pans.

Steamer   A colander placed over a saucepan will act as a steamer.

Straining   When straining fat, line the strainer with a paper tissue to gather up the bits of food and make cleaning easier.

When straining liquid into a bowl through muslin, use spring clothes pegs to hold the muslin securely to the edge of the bowl.

Sweets   When making sweets for a bazaar, use sugar tongs to handle them and keep them unmarked.

Syrup will run easily off a spoon which has been heated before use.

Sprinkle flour on the scales pan before weighing syrup to stop it from sticking. Alternatively, stand the syrup tin on the scales and note the total weight, then take out the required amount of syrup, judging your accuracy by the reduction in the total weight.

Tea cosy   A layer of aluminium foil in the tea cosy lining will help to retain the heat of a teapot.

Teapots   When storing silver or metal teapots, put a cube of sugar or some fresh tea leaves inside to avoid mustiness.

Put an old glove finger over the spout of a teapot not in regular use.

Prevent cracks forming inside a new earthenware teapot by putting it before use into a pan of cold water and bringing it slowly to the boil.

Thermometer   Protect a thermometer from cracking when making jam or sweets by standing it in hot water before and after use.

Tins   To avoid injury when opening a meat tin, hold it with a folded tea cloth as you take out the meat, which will be easier if you have opened it at both ends.

Before storing food tins away, grease the top and bottom slightly with Vaseline to keep them rust-free.

Ensure air-tightness of a tin by closing the lid over a sheet of greaseproof paper.

Collect tins of similar size and paint them to make a set of food containers.

Toast   Bread toasted on one side only is often acceptable to someone who cannot cope with harder toasting.

The steam from hot water poured into the grill pan will prevent thin toast from becoming too hard.

Tomatoes   To skin tomatoes, cover them with boiling water for a few minutes then put them into cold water.

Over-ripe tomatoes will regain their firmness if they are put into ice-cold water with salt for a few hours.

Use an egg-rack to store tomatoes.

Green tomatoes will redden if they are placed in a dark warm place, preferably with an apple, for a few days.

Vacuum flasks   Clean and freshen a vacuum flask by filling it with boiling water and one tablespoonful of bicarbonate of soda.

Uncooked rice shaken up in a flask of warm water will clean the flask.

Slip rubber bands around a flask to give a firm grip.

Flasks chilled with ice cubes can be used to keep drinks cold.

Vanilla   For a constant supply of vanilla-flavoured sugar, cut a vanilla pod in half and place the two pieces, cut ends downwards, in a jar of sugar. Top up as you use the sugar.

Vanilla pods can be dried and re-used, if rinsed in cold water after use.

Vegetables   Save fuel by boiling potatoes and other vegetables in the oven when it is in use for other baking. Put them into boiling water in a lidded dish.

Reduce steam and smells by draining off the hot water in which vegetables have been cooked into a bowl of cold water.

Save cooking time by cutting vegetables into small pieces and save fuel by cooking several vegetables together. Handle-less cups are useful for separating them in the saucepan.

An airy holder for vegetables can be made from an old string vest with the bottom hems stitched together. Hang it up.

Walnuts   Crush shelled walnuts inside a bag with a rolling pin.

Watercress   Keep watercress fresh by standing it in a bowl of water with the stalks uppermost.

Water heating   A kettle of water will become partially heated if left standing over the pilot light on a cooker and will take less fuel to boil when it is needed.

Make additional use of oven heat by placing a dish of water on the bottom of the oven for washing-up.

Whisk   Prevent splashes when you whisk by covering the basin with a plastic bag or a piece of card with a hole in it for the whisk.

Clean a whisk by rotating it under a running tap and using a bottle brush to clear food particles.

Cleaning
Carpets to kettles

How sad that the most beautiful season of the year should be so closely identified with cheerless chores. Summer sunshine . . . autumn tints . . . winter wonderlands . . . but, spring-cleaning.

It seems that, with the first rustle of spring in the air, our great-grandmothers had to think of something to keep all those servants more than fully occupied in their Victorian dust-traps and spring-cleaning was their answer. Turn out everything, shake it, beat it, wash it, polish it and then put it all back again.

For some reason this spring ritual still lingers on in spite of the advent of vacuum cleaners, insect repellents, lighter furniture, washable fabrics, central heating and smaller houses and in spite of the disappearance of domestic helps.

During the winter months there are fewer distractions to lure us from the routine daily and weekly tasks of dusting, vacuuming and general cleaning. So, why should we join the maddening spring chorus of 'This house is filthy – let spring-cleaning begin!'?

I find that the enemy invades my home later on in the year when I succumb to the sun's invitation to laze, when the family is on holiday and when visitors make more attractive demands upon my time.

It is then that the dust settles in the unseen corners, then that garden grit and beach sand become embedded in the carpets. It is then that sticky fingers and spilt drinks do most damage.

Why fling carpets out into the spring sunshine before the moths have laid their eggs? Rather, choose a fine autumn day and, if they have made a home in your carpet, all the young grubs will pop out to frolic in the sunlight only to be annihilated before they start their feast upon your fibres.

And take paint-cleaning. There's nothing like a miserable damp day in November to speed up the process for you. The moist atmosphere loosens the dirt before you begin so that washing down the paintwork becomes child's play.

Why have a chimney swept when fires are still necessary? I like to have mine clean and free of soot when they are out of action in the summer, with no fear of a fall of soot on a damp or windy day. And, of course, you arrange for the sweep to come to suit your convenience instead of his own extremely tight schedule.

The time to cast a clout grows later every year. What point is there in turning out drawers and cupboards in March? There's little hope then of being able to store away the winter woollies, but drawers bulging with summer's untidiness are a challenge worth tackling in October.

We all vary in our vital statistics, in the number and ages of our families, our meal requirements, our shopping facilities, the size of our homes and the amount of time we can, or want to, spend on housekeeping.

Of course, every part of a home needs attention at intervals but, just as you will allocate weekly jobs to be done on appropriate days, so you can spread the bigger undertakings throughout the year to suit your individual way of life.

Work is always more pleasant when you can wait for the right opportunity to do it and, as those who enjoy full-time home-making know, one of its attractions is being able to do things when you want to and not when a rigid timetable forces you into it.

Aluminium saucepans Invert a burnt saucepan over another pan of boiling water, letting it simmer until the burnt food can be easily removed.

Boil apple, rhubarb or lemon parings in aluminium saucepans to remove staining.

When bottling fruit or boiling puddings, add a little vinegar to the water in the saucepan to prevent discoloration.

Animal hairs clinging to upholstery or clothing can be removed easily with foam rubber sponge or with wide Sellotape wrapped, sticky side outwards, around several fingers.

Ashpan Keep coal-fire dust under control on a windy day by carrying the ashpan to the dustbin inside a carrier bag.

Make less dust by separating the cinders from the ashes as they fall by shaping a piece of wire-netting to fit the ashpan and hold the cinders for re-use.

Ashtrays A sprinkling of baking powder in an ashtray will reduce the smell of stale tobacco.

Leave a saucer of ammonia in a room overnight to sweeten it after cigarette smoking.

Bathroom Train the family to give the bath a quick rub down after use to avoid the need for strenuous cleaning.

Supply a long-handled brush, a foam rubber dish-mop or a nylon scouring pad to apply the cleaning powder or washing-up liquid according to the need.

In soft water areas, a foam rubber bag filled with soap scraps will suffice to clean a bath. Users of bath salts and bubble baths, for which soda and washing-up liquid will substitute, need only swill down the bath with clean water.

Paraffin will restore sparkle to a badly neglected bath.

Excess steam in the bathroom damages wallpaper, furnishings and hair-styles. You can minimize the steaminess by turning on the cold water tap first when running a bath.

A band of emulsion paint along the edges of a bathroom mirror will cover up any deterioration caused by condensation.

Use a bottle brush to clean the handbasin overflow passage and a discarded toothbrush to remove the scale which forms around the tap fittings.

Salt mixed with turpentine or rubbed on with lemon skin will remove brown drip marks.

In a carpeted bathroom, a dampened paper towel will pick up the dust which the vacuum cleaner may not reach around pipes and pedestals.

Bedroom cleaning is less trouble if a separate supply of materials and equipment can be stored upstairs.

Bed-springs   Dusty coils attract moths so if you cannot suck out the fluff with your vacuum cleaner, blow it out with a hairdryer. A foam rubber dish-mop is ideal for washing the springs.

Brass ornaments can be brushed clean with a mixture of salt and vinegar.

Soak brass curtain rings and hooks in boiling water and ammonia for about half an hour to remove tarnish.

Rub newly-polished brass with paraffin, furniture cream, petroleum jelly or Vaseline to preserve the shine, or make it last indefinitely with a coating of clear varnish.

Bronze   Clean bronze ornaments with soap and water and polish them with furniture cream.

Brooms and brushes should be washed regularly in warm soapy water with ammonia or soda crystals added, then rinsed well with salt in the final water to stiffen the bristles.

A comb with wide teeth, a skewer and a knitting needle are all useful for removing accumulated fluff from brushes.

A worn-out broom-head can be covered with soft cloth to make an energy-saving polisher.

Buckets   Use two buckets, one of suds and one of clear water, for washing floors or paintwork to save time and materials. Stand each bucket on a tray so that it will slide easily from one position to another.

Candlegrease   Boiling water will remove candlegrease from metal candlesticks.

Candlegrease on wood should be scraped off when it has hardened and the mark cleared with furniture polish.

Cane seat   To tighten a cane chair seat which is sagging in the middle, scrub the seat with hot soapy water, rinse in salted water and dry it in the sunshine, or blow it dry with a hairdryer.

Carpets   Brighten faded colours in a carpet by adding ammonia to the cleaning suds, rinsing it well with clear water.

Keep an egg-whisk in the water when cleaning carpets to maintain a supply of lather and to keep the carpet as dry as possible.

Chamois leathers   After use, wash a chamois leather with soap, pull it into shape and leave it to dry naturally without rinsing.

Soften a hardened leather with a drop of glycerine or olive oil in the water.

Stitch pairs of old chamois leather gloves together through the palms, then slit all the seams to create a mop for window cleaning.

Wear old chamois leather gloves on the hand as dusters for difficult corners and carved furniture.

Chewing gum on fabric can be loosened with carbon tetrachloride, with egg-white on washable material, or it can be chilled hard in the freezer or with an ice cube and then scraped away with a knife.

Chimneys   Reduce soot deposits in the chimney by burning potato peelings mixed with salt regularly.

China   Rub away tea and coffee stains on cups and saucers with a cloth dipped in salt, or soak them in a bleach solution.

Chromium fittings on household appliances can be protected from rust with furniture cream or with a smearing of Vaseline.

Combs will clean easily if scrubbed with a nail-brush in soapy water to which a little ammonia has been added.

Copper can be cleaned with ammonia, with vinegar and salt or with a lemon dipped in salt. It can be lacquered to give it a permanent brilliance.

Decanters   To clean, put a crushed egg-shell, sand, wet tea leaves, small pieces of newspaper or a mixture of salt and vinegar into a stained bottle or decanter and shake it up well with water.

Door mat   Lay a sheet of paper underneath a door mat to make it easy to remove the dust which falls through.

Drains   For quick cleaning and sterilization, place a drain grating on top of a blazing fire until the greasy deposits have burned off. Then lift it carefully on to a shovel with a poker and take it outside to cool before putting it back in place.

A solution of hot water and soda crystals poured down the kitchen sink weekly will keep pipes and drains clean.

Dustbins must be kept clean and fresh to discourage flies. After emptying, rinse your dustbin out with disinfectant and turn it on its side to dry. Line it with newspaper or a large plastic bin liner and wrap up all refuse before putting it into the dustbin.

Rinse all tins and bottles before throwing them away.

A quick way to sterilize a metal dustbin is to burn waste paper in it.

Dusting   You can save time when dusting by working with a duster in each hand and by using a warmed duster for polishing.

A disused baby's hairbrush or a paint brush will clear the dust out of crevices and carvings.

If you add some paraffin to the rinsing water when washing dusters, they will polish as you dust and also deter flies.

To save time on washing dusters, secrete rolls of kitchen paper throughout the house for quick dusting and mopping-up operations.

Similarly, before discarding cotton T-shirts, underpants or any item of absorbent material, use them as dusters or polishers until they are thoroughly dirty and then throw them away.

To pick up every speck of dust when sweeping a floor, press one edge of a dampened sheet of newspaper to the floor and the other edge to the lip of the dustpan.

Egg stains   Rub egg-stained spoons with salt or leave them to soak in the water in which the eggs were boiled.

Electricity fittings   White plastic electric plugs can be cleaned with silver polish. Sockets and switches can be cleaned similarly but you must switch off the electricity supply at the mains beforehand.

Equipment   Make a container on the shoe bag principle from deck-chair canvas or strong linen with pockets designed for various cleaning materials and cloths. Tack it to the inside of a cupboard door.

Keep individual sets of cleaning equipment in plastic peg-baskets and fix a wooden rod across a cupboard to hold them.

Old pillow-cases with a long-handled mop pushed inside are ideal for sweeping down walls and ceilings.

Save old string vests to cut up for dish-cloths and use lock-knit cotton garments for floor-cloths. Terylene net also makes useful dish-cloths and pan-cleaners.

Face-cloths should be boiled regularly in water with vinegar or borax to keep them sweet and free from slime.

Fingermarks on wallpaper can be removed with a piece of white bread.

On doors and furniture, rub fingermarks with a cloth dipped in paraffin, rinsing well afterwards. Furniture polish will give paintwork some resistance to marking.

Fireplace   Cover scorch marks on tiles with a paste of scouring powder and leave until dry when the mark will wash off.

Brighten the appearance of a hearth by leaving a thin covering of white scouring powder in the grouting between the tiles when you wash them, or paint the grouting with white shoe cleaner.

Fluffy toys can be dry-cleaned by shaking them up in a bag with some borax and then brushing it out.

Forks   Use a pipe-cleaner to apply silver polish between the prongs of forks.

Frying pans The kitchen cooker will require less cleaning if you cover the frying pan with a lid or a colander.

Gas burners Use a pipe cleaner to clear a blocked gas burner.

Burnt-on deposits on gas burners can be removed by soaking them in a hot soapy soda or ammonia solution.

Grease Soak up grease spilt on polished surfaces at once with paper tissues, then wash the area with warm soapy water and polish it with furniture cream.

Grease on the floor should be left to set (which can be hastened with an ice cube) and then scraped off with a knife. Carpeting should then have a hot iron applied to it over blotting-paper, the treatment continuing until all the grease has been removed. Finally, wash with warm suds and ammonia and rinse well.

For grease on wallpaper and upholstery, first try the blotting-paper-and-warm-iron treatment. If unsuccessful, make a paste of carbon tetrachloride and starch or french chalk and leave this on overnight before brushing it off.

Eucalyptus oil will remove grease marks from upholstery and clothing.

Heat marks To remove heat marks from polished surfaces, wash off any accumulated polish before rubbing the affected area only with one of the following: metal polish, camphorated oil, cigarette ash, methylated spirits, butter or Vaseline. Re-polish the entire surface.

Hide furniture can be cleaned with equal parts of warm water and vinegar and then treated with hide polish.

Ivory benefits from exposure to sunshine, so leave your piano keyboard open and wash the keys occasionally with milk.

Jewellery can be brightened by washing it in warm suds with a little ammonia, using a soft toothbrush to penetrate the crevices. A diamond can be cleaned with a little gin.

Spectacle lens cleaning tissue will also polish jewellery.

A piece of camphor or chalk will prevent tarnishing if kept in a jewellery box.

Kettle fur can be loosened by boiling a solution of one tablespoonful of borax to one pint of water in the kettle, rinsing it well afterwards.

In hard water areas, keep a piece of loofah or a small pebble in the kettle to prevent furring.

Kneeling mat An old hot water bottle stuffed with shredded nylons or newspapers makes a waterproof kneeling mat.

Lenses can be cleaned and polished with newspaper which has been crumpled and then smoothed flat.

Mica windows on stoves can be cleaned with metal polish but only when the fire is not burning because the polish is highly inflammable.

Mildew on books will sometimes brush off but, if it persists, sprinkle the pages with chalk or starch and brush this off after several days.
   Fresh air and sunshine will banish the smell of mildew.
   Mildew on fabric is difficult to remove, on white articles such as handkerchiefs try using a strong bleach solution.

Milk bottles are easier to clean if rinsed first in cold water.

Moquette   Brush furniture upholstered in moquette with a stiff nylon brush when vacuuming it. Remove any spots with ammonia in soapy water.

Mouldings   Use an old toothbrush to get into the corners of mouldings and window frames when washing them.

Ornaments   Wash china, pottery and glass ornaments in warm soapy water and ammonia to make them sparkle.

Ovens need to be wiped down while still hot with a damp, soapy cloth, using scouring powder to remove any burnt-on deposits.
   Clean around the control knobs with a pipe-cleaner or with rag wrapped around a cocktail stick.
   Line the oven base with disposable aluminium foil to save cleaning time and labour.

Ovenware   Clean stains on glass ovenware by soaking it in a hot soapy ammonia or soda solution.

Paintwork   Work upwards when washing paintwork to avoid streaks, then dry it downwards.
   Tie a band of towelling around your wrist when washing ceilings to absorb the drips.
   Choose a damp day when you wash paintwork as the moist atmosphere loosens the dirt and grease and makes the work much easier. But, if the sun persists in shining, you can achieve the same effect indoors by leaving a kettle steaming in the room before you begin.
   Keep your clean paintwork looking that way longer by coating it with silicone polish straight away. Window-sills, in particular, benefit from this treatment.

Parquet floors should be cleaned with turpentine and the stains removed with steel wool. Finish with a wax polish.

Playing cards can be cleaned with bread or by gently sponging with milk.

Polishing Dusters soaked in a mixture of one teaspoonful of furniture cream to a quarter of a pint of water, then dried, will polish as they dust.

A damp cloth will spread polish more economically than a dry one.

Polish will be easier to apply if the tin is slightly warmed before you use it.

Pour a little vinegar on hardened shoe or floor polish to soften it.

Prams Avoid muddy wheel-marks indoors by making slip-on covers for pram wheels from large plastic bags.

Protect chromium and other metal on a pram in the winter months by smearing it with lubricating oil or Vaseline.

When treating the chromium levers on the hood, hold a piece of cardboard or a folded newspaper between them and the hood to keep it unmarked.

Liquid suede cleaner will renovate a fading fabric hood.

Refrigerator This should be washed inside after de-frosting with a solution of two teaspoonfuls of bicarbonate of soda to one pint of water to clean and purify it. A hairdryer will complete the drying process before you switch it on again.

Rubber heel marks on linoleum and vinyl floor coverings can be removed with turpentine.

Scouring powder Block up some of the holes in a tin of scouring powder for more economical control of the amount used.

Scrubbing brushes Screw a door knob or a drawer handle to a scrubbing brush to give a good grip and to protect your hands.

Shoe cleaning A crown cork nailed to the back of a shoe-brush will scrape mud off shoes.

A piece of perforated zinc, cut to size and placed on top of shoe polish in a tin, will control the supply and prevent lumps of polish from spilling out of the tin.

Wear old woollen mittens when cleaning shoes to protect your hands and to give the shoes a final polish.

White liquid shoe cleaner can be coloured with poster or water paints to match a fabric shoe.

Scratches on brown shoes can be painted out with iodine and those on white shoes with typing correction fluid. Other colours can often be matched with a felt pen.

You can encourage young children to clean their own shoes by applying the polish yourself at night and letting them brush on a shine in the morning.

Silverware should be washed as soon as possible after use and dried thoroughly.

Cutlery kept in a dry air-tight box will not need cleaning as often as that exposed to moist air. Items not in frequent use will remain untarnished if you wrap them in aluminium foil, tissue paper or a plastic bag to exclude the air.

Display cabinets can be made air-tight with strips of self-adhesive plastic foam.

Toothpaste acts as a gentle cleaner for delicate silverware. Apply it with a soft damp cloth.

Put some milk bottle tops or silver paper into a jar of salted water and keep it beside the sink for stained spoons and forks. Dip them in briefly and rinse well.

Make a silver cloth by soaking a tea towel in a solution of half a pint of ammonia to one heaped tablespoonful of plate powder, leaving it to drip dry. Use it as a stain remover and polisher.

Smoky patches on the ceiling and walls above the fireplace can be lightened by applying a paste of thick starch, brushing it off when dry.

Soot marks on carpets can be removed with carbon tetrachloride, but keep doors and windows open as you use it.

Sprinkle a sooty rug well with salt and take it outdoors to give it a thorough brushing.

Sponges   Clean a sponge by soaking it in salted water or in vinegar and water, replacing the solution as the slime extrudes until the sponge is quite clear. If the sponge is rinsed well in clear water after each use the problem will not arise.

Steel wool   Prevent pads of steel wool from rusting by covering them with soapy water when not in use, or wrapping them in foil.

Boxes of soap-filled steel wool pads will last longer if you use only one-third of a pad at a time.

Straw baskets   Soak a sagging straw basket in salted cold water to revive it.

Tar stains   Scrape away as much solid tar as possible, rub in lard or Vaseline and scrub the stain well with warm soapy water and ammonia. Eucalyptus oil, turpentine or carbon tetrachloride will remove stubborn stains.

Teapots   Fill stained china or earthenware teapots with a bleach solution or with a biological washing powder solution and leave until the stains have vanished.

Metal teapots can be cleaned with a solution of one tablespoonful of borax to one pint of boiling water left for several hours and then rinsed well.

Telephones   Use a small painting brush to clean the dust out of a telephone dial.

Wash the dial face by wrapping a small piece of cotton wool around the blunt end of a ballpoint pen and dialling O with it several times.

Upholstery   Control the dust when beating upholstery indoors by covering the article being cleaned with a dampened dust sheet.

Urine stains on carpets or upholstery can be removed by sponging them with vinegar and water.

Vacuum cleaners   Disposable paper bags can be emptied carefully and re-used several times. A large paper bag fastened around a deteriorating disposable bag will give it even longer life.

Glue magnets to the front of a vacuum cleaner so that you can pick up small metallic objects before they are sucked inside.

Vases   If you line a flower vase with a plastic bag to hold the water, it will be easier to clean.

Clear stains from vases with a bleach solution or with a denture cleaning tablet.

Venetian blinds   Wear an old cotton glove or use a foam rubber dish-mop to clean the slats of venetian blinds. For a thorough cleaning, immerse the blind in soap suds in the bath.

Vinegar bottles can be cleaned by shaking up tea leaves in them to remove the staining.

Wallpaper   Dust embossed patterns with old net curtaining.

Wardrobe tops are easier to clean if you cover them with wallpaper or floor covering which can be taken down to dust or discard.

Washing-up   In hard water areas, a few drops of ammonia or a few soda crystals will soften the water and help to dispel grease.

When only a few dishes have to be washed, use a smaller washing-up bowl, or a mixing bowl, for economy in hot water and washing-up liquid.

Wastepipes   Before going away on holiday, force a mixture of salt and soda into the bathroom wastepipes. On your return, a kettle of boiling water poured down the pipes will clear away the accumulated slime which has been released in your absence. But be careful when treating the handbasin wastepipe, boiling water can crack cold porcelain.

The kitchen wastepipe needs a weekly cleaning with boiling water and soda crystals.

Use expanding curtain wire with a hook on the end to clear a blocked sink.

Water marks   Marks made by wet glasses on wooden surfaces should be left to dry out thoroughly for several weeks. The rings can then be darkened by rubbing in butter, Vaseline or shoe polish.

White shoes   In an emergency, white scouring powder or talcum powder applied liberally to canvas shoes will substitute for whitening.

White socks   Stubborn marks on socks can also be hidden with talcum powder.

Windows   Smear kitchen windows with glycerine or with a mixture of equal parts of glycerine and methylated spirits to reduce misting.

Crumpled newspaper will mop up condensation on windows.

In winter, leave a strip of folded newspaper on window ledges to soak up the condensation drips or melting frost.

A pad of newspaper dipped in paraffin or methylated spirits will clean a window and deter flies.

Make your own window-cleaning mixture from equal parts of paraffin, methylated spirits and water, shaken up in a plastic squirter bottle for easy application.

Window stickers   Nail polish remover will clear the stickiness left by labels and posters stuck on windows.

Wine stains on upholstery and carpets should be sponged with one tablespoonful of borax to half a litre of warm water. *See also* **Stains**.

Washing and Ironing
Chiffon to shirts

'When you grow up, there will be washing machines. They have them already in America!'

To my shame, I laughed in scornful disbelief at my mother's words, as she rubbed away with a bar of soap at a zinc bath on the kitchen table. In my young mind, her fantastic prediction conjured up at once a picture of large oval baths, each fitted with a dozen human arms. And perhaps because, characteristically, she made light work of a weekly wash for eight of us, I could see no need for such a foreign intrusion into our domestic scene and therefore, quite illogically, no likelihood of such an invention.

If I ever had to take part in a 'Desert Island Detergents' exercise, I would opt without hesitation for a bar of humble household soap in preference to the miracle machines and soapless wonders of today.

For those items which need individual attention, I still find bar soap irreplaceable on wash-day. It speedily whitens children's muddy socks, rubs away lipstick and other greasy stains, cleans collars and cuffs and, given time, it will even ease out paint splashes on clothing. And, in the process, work-stained hands are cleaned and softened, without even trying.

I admitted, at a recent gathering, that I enjoy hand-washing, elbow-deep in soap-suds at the sink. It may be simply that I have never outgrown a child's inborn love of water-play, but I often wash small amounts in this way telling myself that it saves time and the extravagant hot-water demands of a full washer.

My friends were aghast.

'I just wouldn't know how to begin washing by hand,' one said. 'All I want is to push things into that hole and flick a switch!'

I wonder whether some mother of the future will say to her child, as she laboriously works out which switch she should press, 'When you grow up, you'll be able to wash by hand. They're doing it already in America!'

Airing   Increase the capacity of an airing cupboard by fixing towel rails or plastic-covered curtain wire to the inside of the door and underneath the shelves. These also help to keep blouses and shirts crease-free.

Aprons   Stitch a length of plastic material, about twelve inches deep, to the reverse side of fabric apron waistbands for protection against splashes on wash-day.

If you use a plastic apron, stitch a wide band of towelling across the bottom to absorb the drips.

When washing aprons, tie the strings together to prevent tangling in the washing machine and, when hanging them up to dry, flatten out the strings to make ironing quicker.

Ballpoint pen marks can be removed with methylated spirits or nail varnish remover. *See also* **Stains**.

A typewriter rubber will remove ballpoint pen marks from suede.

Berets   To retain the shape of a beret, dry it after washing by stretching it over a plate of similar size.

Blankets   To keep woollen blankets soft, add glycerine to the last rinsing water.

You can brighten a discoloured blanket with a cold-water dye.

Cardigans   Before you wash a heavy cardigan, fasten the buttons and tack the back and fronts together at the welt to help it retain its shape.

Chiffon   Rinse chiffon in a weak solution of starch and iron it while damp to restore its crispness. Iron it over a damp cloth if it has become too dry.

Chocolate stains should be soaked in a borax solution before washing. *See also* **Stains**.

Clothes basket   The bottom of the clothes basket will keep clean when standing outside if you fasten four cotton reels to the base to make feet for it.

Clothes freshener   Freshen suits and dresses by sponging them with a solution of one teaspoonful of ammonia to one pint of warm water and hanging them in the fresh air to dry.

Clothes line   Boil a new rope clothes line before using it so that it will not stretch in use.

To clean a clothes line without tangling it, wind it around a piece of board for scrubbing and leave it there to dry.

When drying garments on coat-hangers, make a knot in the line and slip the hook of the hanger through it to keep it secure, or fasten the hanger to the line with string or a pipe cleaner.

To prevent a wooden hanger from staining wet garments, cover it with aluminium foil or a plastic bag. Do the same with a metal hanger to prevent rusting.

When drip-drying, put a large plastic bag over a coat-hanger and hang garments over this for quicker and smoother drying.

Avoid peg-marks on jumpers and dresses by passing an old pair of tights through the sleeves and pegging the tights to the line at the toes and waist.

For space economy, set up a pair of parallel clothes lines, a short distance apart, and fasten articles from one line to the other.

Another space economy is to peg small items such as socks and handkerchiefs to the bar of a wire coat-hanger.

Save time by folding garments as you take them off the line and make use of a pillow-case to hold small items.

Clothes pegs   Keep your clothes pegs in an old handbag or a child's bucket so that you can slide it along the line as you work.

An old shoulder bag also makes a useful peg container.

Clothes-prop   Cover your clothes-prop with an old stocking to protect garments which blow against it.

Keep the prop under control on a windy day by boring a hole through each side of the V-shaped top so that a piece of dowelling can be slipped through it to keep the line secure.

A plastic tub embedded in the lawn will hold the prop steady and protect the lawn.

Cocoa and **Coffee stains** should be soaked in a borax solution before washing. *See also* **Stains**.

Collars   When a collar has become too dry for ironing, the steam from a kettle will soon produce the right degree of dampness.

Rub heavily-soiled collars and cuffs with moist soap and leave overnight to soak. A nylon scouring pad is useful for gently scrubbing them clean.

To keep newly-ironed collars uncreased, push a cotton reel on to the base of a coat-hanger hook.

Coloured articles   If you are in doubt about the colour fastness of a fabric, soak it in a solution of one tablespoonful of salt to one gallon of water before you wash it.

Corduroy will dry without creases if you hang it to drip-dry and brush the garment downwards in line with the ridges.

Curtains   Curtain lining often soils more quickly than the curtain, especially if it is near an open window. If you attach the lining by press studs instead of stitching you can take it down and wash it separately.

When ironing large curtains, iron a wide strip up the centre of the curtain to avoid making a crease when it is folded.

A bath cube dissolved in the final rinsing water freshens net curtains and gets rid of the dusty smell which sometimes persists even after washing.

Protect kitchen curtains from splashes on wash-day by tying a plastic bag loosely around the ends.

Cushion covers made with a zip fastener or self-sticking tape or in the style of a pillow case will save you time when you launder them.

Dampening   Keep a moistened foam rubber sponge beside the ironing board for dampening articles which have become too dry for ironing. A polythene squirter bottle filled with water is also useful for this purpose.

Keep damp articles awaiting ironing in a plastic bag, but not for too long because mildew could occur.

Dyeing   To ensure that no specks of the powder remain undissolved in a hot water dye, boil the dye powder first in a small amount of the total quantity of water required. Then pour it through a strainer, lined with a paper tissue, to add it to the full quantity of water.

When dyeing articles, it is a good idea to dye a length of white sewing cotton at the same time.

A tea infuser makes a useful holder for a tinting cube.

Egg stains in fabric should be soaked in cold water with a little salt before washing. *See also* **Stains**.

Embroidery   Place embroidered table linen on a bath towel and iron it on the wrong side.

Frozen washing   If you hang out washing in sub-zero temperatures, put salt in the final rinsing water to stop it freezing.

Fruit stains should be soaked in a borax solution or glycerine before washing. *See also* **Stains**.

Gloves   Keep fabric gloves on your hands to wash them. Starch them afterwards to make them dirt-resistant.

Grass stains should be sponged with methylated spirits or soaked in glycerine before washing. *See also* **Stains**.

Guest towels   Keep a roll of patterned kitchen paper in the bathroom for use as guest towels.

Hair ribbons can be quickly smoothed flat on the top of a hot kettle or saucepan or on the stovepipe of a kitchen boiler. When not in use, wind them around empty cotton reels and secure them with Sellotape.

Handkerchiefs   Soak heavily-soiled handkerchiefs in cold salted water overnight to dissolve the mucus and then boil them. One teaspoonful of borax added to a pan of water will help to keep them a good colour.

Tear up discarded sheets and any soft cotton material to make disposable handkerchiefs for heavy colds.

Ink stains on fabrics should be rinsed with cold water immediately and left to soak in milk and salt. Any remaining stain can be cleared with a mild bleach solution on suitable fabrics. *See also* **Stains**.

Irons   Brown marks on the base of an iron can be rubbed off with soap, salt or cleaning paste while the iron is still warm, but always unplug it first.

Clear blocked holes in a steam iron with a pipe cleaner.

To smooth a small conspicuous crease without removing the garment, use a heated tablespoon as a substitute iron.

Ironing boards   To avoid any danger to children when ironing, screw a shallow baking tin to the ironing board to hold the iron securely.

A layer of aluminium foil fixed beneath the ironing-board cover will contain the heat and speed the ironing.

Use the legs of old pyjama trousers for ironing-board covers.

Fasten a strong plastic bag beneath your ironing board to hold pressing cloths and a needle and cotton.

Iron mould   Cream of tartar will remove iron mould stains from white articles if rubbed in well with a piece of lemon. Household bleach can also be used. Rinse well and dry in sunshine.

Jeans are easy to wash if you lay them, folded, on the draining board and scrub each side with a nail brush.

Lace   Iron lace over darker material to show up the edging and cover the lace with tissue paper to avoid a shiny finish.

Lipstick stains can be loosened with glycerine, lard or Vaseline before washing with bar soap.

White bread will rub away a slight lipstick mark. *See also* **Stains**.

Nappies   Reduce nappy soiling by cutting a large roll of cellulose wadding into 20 cm squares. If you place one of these inside the nappy, it will absorb the bulk of the soiling and can be destroyed.

Nappies smelling of ammonia can be freshened by soaking them in a pail of water with two tablespoonfuls of vinegar. Rinse well afterwards.

A little glycerine in the final rinsing water will keep nappies soft.

Net curtains will dry without creases if they are not wrung out after rinsing but put straight on the line to drip-dry, or they can be threaded onto a plastic clothes line.

If a net curtain is out of shape after drying, push a rod through the bottom hem and leave it hanging in the curtain for a few days to straighten it.

Add a small amount of glue size to the final rinsing water to stiffen net curtains.

Perspiration marks should be sponged with a weak solution of vinegar or ammonia and water.

Plastic pants   Glycerine in the rinsing water will keep a baby's plastic pants in good condition.

Pleats   To keep a pleated skirt in good shape when washing it, fold it lengthways and pull it through a footless nylon stocking.

Pressing   Use newspaper instead of an ironing cloth for pressing sweaters and trousers.

When pressing seams, slip folded newspaper under the seam edges to avoid the unsightly mark which would otherwise occur on the outside of the garment.

A folded towel or a rolled magazine will act as a sleeve board. For sleeve-heads, hold a thick pad of towelling inside when pressing.

Pullovers   To speed the drying of a heavy-knit pullover, stuff it with crumpled newspaper, which should be replaced as it becomes sodden.

Scorch marks   Exposure to sunshine will remove slight scorching if you continually dampen the article, as it dries, with salted water.

Heavier scorching can be treated with onion juice, a paste of borax and glycerine, hydrogen peroxide or a mild bleach solution. Speedy treatment helps.

Sheets   Avoid total disaster to your sheets when pegs are blown off the line on a windy day by hanging the sheets over the line and placing spring-clip pegs down the sides of the sheet, or by fastening the two sides of the sheet together with large safety-pins.

If you fold sheets when taking them off the line and stack them in a neat pile, they will be less trouble to iron. If they have blown out of shape on the line, fold them in four and jam one end in a drawer so that you can pull sharply until the sheet has regained its shape.

Use folded sheets as a cover for the ironing board and iron the other items first over the sheets, so that they will require little ironing themselves.

Shiny patches   Sponge a shiny patch on trousers or a skirt with ammonia and water or press it under a very damp cloth with a hot iron, brushing the fabric gently with a rubber suede brush to raise the pile. Very fine sandpaper can be used as an alternative on heavy fabrics.

A skirt with a shiny seat can be unpicked and made up again with the material reversed.

Shirts   Shirt sleeves will not tangle with other garments in the washing machine if you fasten the cuffs to the front buttons.

Sinks When washing articles in the sink, cover the plug with a plastic mat so that it will not be loosened inadvertently.

Soap powder Prevent soap powder packets from disintegrating through dampness by fitting them inside a plastic bag, or transfer the powder into an empty glass jar.

Scraps of soap can be shredded in the mincing machine and used in the washing machine with soap powder.

To dispense powder economically, make two small holes in the top of the packet to use instead of the usual side opening. The holes can be plugged to avoid wastage from spills.

The foam from soapless detergents will disappear quickly if you rub a tablet of soap in it.

Socks Remove brown marks from socks by soaking them in salted water and rubbing them with bar soap.

Discoloured white socks can be given new life with a change of colour by dyeing them in cold tea, or dye.

Stains In the bewildering world of today's man-made fibres, it is a relief to find, when tackling stains, that most garments now bear details of the composition of their fabric and that most of them are washable.

The best first-aid treatment for non-greasy stains on washable material is immediate immersion in cold water. When in doubt about the washability of a fabric, mop up liquid with tissues, blotting paper or towelling and scrape off solid matter, such as tar, before experimenting with the cleaning agent on an inconspicuous area of the fabric or taking it to a dry cleaner.

Soap and lukewarm water will remove many stains with the added power, if needed, of one tablespoonful of borax to half a litre of water.

Carbon tetrachloride removes grease and oil stains from cotton, wool, nylon and Terylene fabrics, but the vapour must not be inhaled, so keep your doors or windows open when you use it. French chalk, starch and talcum powder will soak up grease. Glycerine, Vaseline and lard will loosen hardened stains prior to washing or treatment with a solvent.

It is a good idea to hold a pad of towelling or other absorbent material over the area and push the stain out of the fabric by working from the wrong side of the material. Work also from the outer edges of the stain to avoid a ring-marking. (*See also* Index under '**Stains**'.)

Starch Prevent a skin forming on newly-made starch by adding cold water immediately to dilute it to the required consistency.

If your starch becomes lumpy, whip it smooth with an egg-whisk.

Add a little glycerine to starch to prevent it sticking to the iron.

Store left-over starch in a polythene squirter bottle and use it to dampen dry ironing.

43

Suede   Revive shabby suede jackets and skirts by hanging them in a steamy bathroom before treatment with a suede brush.

Tea stains should be soaked in a borax solution before washing. *See also* **Stains**.

Ties   Before washing a tie, tack down each side with cotton and leave this in until you have ironed the tie.

For a crease-free finish when pressing a tie, fold a sheet of newspaper or cut cardboard to its shape and insert this in the tie. Use a ruler for the thin end.

Trousers   To obtain a long-lasting crease in trousers, rub the inside of the creases with bar soap or spray them with starch before pressing them.

Underwear   Keep toilet soap and empty perfume bottles in your undies drawer.

Veils   Hair lacquer will stiffen a limp veil.

Velours   Freshen a velours hat by brushing it over a steaming kettle.

Velvet   Creased velvet dresses and suits will become smooth again if they are hung up in a steamy bathroom.

Remove fluff from velvet with a piece of plastic foam or with a strip of Sellotape wound, sticky side outwards, around several fingers.

Washing machine   Keep a washing machine sweet-smelling when not in use by putting a deodorant block inside.

White necklines   Dust white necklines with white talcum powder to keep them looking fresh.

Wine stains should be soaked in a borax solution before washing. *See also* **Stains**.

Woollens   Remove all traces of soap when rinsing woollens by adding vinegar to the last rinsing water. A little glycerine in the rinsing water will keep woollens soft.

To dry woollens, roll them in a towel, and squeeze out as much water as possible. Then dry them flat, shaping them correctly, in the fresh air. A pram net is ideal for this purpose.

To prevent dark-coloured woollens from picking up fluff from other articles when being washed, turn them inside out.

Yellowing woollens can be whitened in a solution of one part of hydrogen peroxide to ten parts of water.

Wringing   When wringing by hand, and speed is unimportant, labour can be saved by piling the wet washing on top of a dish drainer until the main bulk of the water has drained away.

Making and Mending

Seams to sequins

Apart from those who are dedicated to the needle, most of us acquire the basic principles of sewing and knitting without even noticing, especially if we spent our early years as proud 'mothers' of a family of dolls.

But, even if we by-passed this childhood recreation, we can be certain that at some stage in life we shall be forced by sheer self-preservation to take up a needle and thread and do our best with a split seam, a sagging hem or a loose button.

That may be the extent of our interest in the subject but, as the years go by, the two main items tend to multiply in colours and sizes and the sound sense of keeping a well-furnished sewing box becomes only too apparent.

Sew on a coat button with machine silk and you will have to sew it on again within a few weeks. But sew it on with button thread, properly shanked and with a small button at the back to take the strain, and you will have no more trouble for years.

Today's machine-stitched buttons are notoriously insecure and it is well worth spending time strengthening the button-stitching of all new clothes before you wear them. Too often, if one button is lost, you have to buy an entire new set in replacement.

It is well said that 'a stitch in time saves nine' and one of the handiest places to keep sewing materials is within easy reach of the ironing board. A minute spent at that stage to sew on a button or to strengthen a seam is far less trouble and time-consuming than forcing yourself to face a pile of small mending jobs later on.

Before he left home, I gave my student son a short survival course in the art of sewing on buttons and darning socks. And I tucked a small tin containing cotton reels, cards of wool and various buttons and needles into his trunk. I knew quite well that it would never be opened but I was content that I had done my duty.

When he came home for Christmas, he was wearing an old pair of jeans complete with a brand-new zip-fastener. It was hand-sewn by himself, he casually told me, the outcome of an emergency which had to be met.

Aprons   If the pockets of your apron catch on door handles, wear it inside out. To prevent this nuisance, it is a good idea to stitch pockets diagonally across the reverse side when making an apron.

A wide band of towelling stitched down each side of an apron is very useful for quick hand-drying .

Skirts of discarded summer dresses convert very easily to aprons; the best parts of old plastic tablecloths can be used similarly.

Baby's night-gown   When cutting out a baby's night-gown, allow extra length at the hem so that tape can be threaded through the hem to draw it up to keep baby's feet warm.

Make night-gowns in Magyar style with several tucks on each shoulder which can be let out as your baby grows so that the gowns will last much longer.

Badges   When stitching a badge to a pocket or sleeve, slip a piece of cardboard inside for support.

Belts   Avoid losing belts by stitching them to the centre back of garments.

Bibs   Make a large bib for meal-times from a worn towel by cutting an opening in the centre to fit over the baby's head. The bottom can be turned up to make a pocket to catch falling food.

Blankets made redundant by duvets can be used to make ponchos or capes.

Bolero   When making a summer dress, allow sufficient material to make a matching bolero.

Buttoned openings   Blouses and dresses will look neater if their buttoned openings are finished with a hook and eye at the top.

Buttons   A small button sewn on the inside of a garment behind a larger button will take the strain and prevent the fabric from being torn.

For extra security with four-hole buttons, sew through each pair of holes separately, fastening off the thread each time.

To form a shank easily on coat buttons, place a matchstick between the fabric and the button so that about 5 mm of thread is left for the shank.

Use shirring elastic to sew buttons on children's clothes and on the skirts of button-through dresses.

To help trouser buttons stand more strain, pass the needle through at an angle, using up a larger area behind the button than usual.

Button threads will last longer if you rub them on beeswax before stitching or coat them with nail varnish afterwards.

Matching fabric buttons made on a metal button mould often rust in washing. Prevent this happening by putting a piece of plastic between the fabric and the mould when you make them.

To match knitted cardigan buttons exactly, cover a two-hole button with the knitting wool, sewing over and over from the centre until the button is covered.

Keep matching buttons together by threading them on fuse wire or large safety-pins.

Buttonholes   Knit both fronts of a cardigan on the same needle so that, when a buttonhole is made, an identifying stitch can be made on the other front for the button position.

For firmer knitted buttonholes, after casting on the stitches knit into the backs of the stitches on the next row. They can also be reinforced with hand- or machine-stitching later.

When making a buttonhole on fabric, outline it first with a pencil or tacking and machine-stitch the outline before cutting it for hand-stitching.

Cardigans   A thick-knitted cardigan will hang better and retain its shape if it is lined. Cut out the lining shape from the knitted pieces before sewing them up.

To keep a heavy cardigan in shape when hung up, sew a loop to each underarm seam and hang it from these.

Give new life to a tight knitted cardigan by cutting off the buttons, sewing up the buttonholes and inserting an open-ended zip fastener. Simple embroidery would smarten the front bands, if necessary.

Casting on and off   To ensure a firm and elastic edge, cast on by knitting between the previous two stitches instead of into the previous stitch and cast off with a needle one size larger.

Reinforce welts by knitting into the back of the stitches in the first row.

When picking up stitches at the neck, use a smaller needle to avoid holes.

Collars   When a collar on a white or plain-coloured shirt or blouse becomes worn (but the rest of the garment is in good condition) take off the collar and, using it as a pattern, make a new collar in a contrasting colour or fabric. For example, you could have a needlecord or velvet collar or one made from a striped or flowered material. You could also do the same with the cuffs. This practice could also be used on a dress.

Cot blankets   Use a circular needle for knitting odd balls of wool into a cot blanket. With both ends sewn up, this makes a blanket of double thickness and can be made even warmer by inserting a sheet of plastic foam.

Cotton reels   Keep cotton reels tidy on a knitting needle with a cork on the end to secure them.

Crochet   When working intricate lace motifs, crochet the pattern first in thick cotton and keep it handy as a guide.

Cross stitch   When you are working a cross stitch design on a knitted garment, tack a piece of cross stitch canvas in position and work the design over this. When completed, the canvas can be easily cut and the threads removed.

Cuffs   Sleeves from discarded blouses or jumpers can be cut off, hemmed and threaded with elastic at the elbow to make protective cuffs for long sleeves when working at the sink if your rubber gloves do not give sufficient protection.

Cuffs knitted on four needles look much neater than those knitted on two needles when they are turned back because no seam is visible.

Cushions   Push a small wad of cotton wool into each corner of a cushion cover to give it a firm shape.

Cutting out   To ensure that you have a straight edge for cutting purposes, draw out a thread right across the material and cut along this line.

Pin slippery material together down both sides for accuracy in cutting.

On flimsy materials, outline each pattern piece in soap to prevent fraying.

Instead of cutting out notches, mark them with a pencil or make one slit with scissors for each notch.

Hair-grips and curl-clips are useful for holding a pattern in place without damaging it.

Stiffen limp paper patterns by placing them between two sheets of waxed paper from a cereal packet and pressing them with a warm iron.

Darning   If you are a firm believer in the somewhat dying art of darning add strength to your darn by using matching cotton with the wool.

A lighted battery torch makes a useful 'mushroom' for fine darning.

A piece of net tacked over big holes makes darning easier.

Drawn threads   Threads will pull out easily if the drawn-work area is rubbed with bar soap before starting.

Dresses   To enable a dress to be quickly lengthened, make a tuck in the back of a wide hem when making the dress. It will then be a simple matter to unstitch this and no further sewing will be required.

If you make vertical pin tucks in the bodice of a dress, it can be let out with growth and, if fading or stitching is evident, braid, lace, embroidery or binding can be used to cover it up. These will also hide hem markings or fading when a hem is lengthened.

Dressmaking scraps   Keep fabric remnants in a plastic bag so that you can find the piece you need quickly. Use them for patch work.

Dropped stitches   Use a crochet hook to pick up dropped stitches in knitting.

Dungarees   When you patch the knees of dungarees, use a long piece of contrasting material from the knee to well up the thigh, stitching the knee patch but turning the thigh piece into a pocket.

Dungarees made from an old rubber-backed raincoat will protect a toddler who enjoys playing outside even in wet weather.

Elastic   To renew elastic quickly, join the new length to the old one before you pull it out.

Elbows   When elbows in knitted sweaters or cardigans become thin, sew leather, corduroy or suede patches on to the garment. These are very fashionable and are fairly simple to sew on.

Elbows on new knitwear can be similarly protected with a patch of any soft matching fabric carefully stitched to the *inside*.

Embroidery   When embroidering knitted fabric, tack a piece of soft material behind the design area and stitch right through it to prevent stretching and mis-shaping.

Store embroidery silks in an old book with the ends protruding for easy selection.

A strip of Sellotape over the labels will secure the skeins and also make re-ordering simple.

Foam-backed material   is easier to handle if you stitch the seams over a length of tape.

Friendship cloth   An unusual farewell gift can be made by inviting the recipient's friends to embroider their names on a plain linen cloth.

Gathering   When making a gathered skirt with elastic at the waist-line, you will find that two rows of narrow elastic are more effective than one of wide elastic.

Gloves   To avoid losing them, fasten children's gloves to a length of elastic which can be threaded through the sleeves of any coat they wear.

Fabric gloves can be trimmed with material matching a summer outfit.

Hems   An emergency hem repair can be made with Sellotape.

Hair-grips or paper-clips can be used as an alternative to pins when turning up hems.

To achieve a straight hem-line, use a notched stick to make an even measurement from the floor up to the skirt edge.

Inside pocket   Stitch a zip-fastener or self-sticking looped tape across an inside pocket in a jacket to foil thieves.

Knitting needles   Mark off one needle in each pair in centimetres to make a handy measure.

Cover the size markings on needles with Sellotape or clear nail varnish to keep them easily visible.

Stitches are easier to count if you use needles of a contrasting colour to the wool and they will slide along better if you polish the needles with furniture cream.

Replace a broken knitting needle knob with a toothpaste-tube cap.

A broken needle end can be filed to a point and the new tip treated with nail varnish.

Make a hanging holder for needles from the wide end of a tie, stiffened with cardboard.

When discarding curtains, retain a length of the top section with the curtain tape attached and use this as a needle-holder, slotting the needles through the loops.

If you keep your needles in a box, line it with corrugated paper to keep the needles tidy.

Use a spring-clip clothes peg to secure your knitting when putting it away.

Knitting patterns   Make a pattern easier to follow by putting a coloured marking around the stitch and row numbers which apply to your size.

Protect knitting patterns by fixing them inside a plastic bag. If possible, stick the pattern on card.

To find your place easily when following a complicated pattern, mark the pattern row with a paper-clip or a hair-grip.

Knitting wool   Keep your wool clean when knitting by putting it in a plastic bag loosely closed with a rubber band.

Odd balls of wool stored in a plastic bag will be found quickly when required.

When working a multi-coloured pattern, to avoid tangles pass each strand of wool through a button or a large bead. Plastic bags with holes punched in them, as used for vegetables, or kitchen colanders are useful for this purpose and can be used also for storage.

Laces   It is a good idea to save the good parts from old shoe laces; they make strong loops for hanging coats and can replace broken duffel-coat toggles or button loops.

Leather patches on jackets will be easier to stitch if they are first placed under an unthreaded sewing machine needle and a line of holes is run around the edges.

Linings   Use self-sticking looped tape to fasten detachable linings to coats.

Long dresses often become badly creased at the bottom hem in a wardrobe. To prevent this sew two loops to the inside of the waistband and hang the dress, turned inside out, from these loops.

Loose covers   When making loose covers, include some built-in pockets. A shallow one is useful on the inside of a chair arm for knitting or spectacles and a deep one on the outside for newspapers and magazines.

Use Velcro instead of tapes to secure loose covers to a chair.

You can help new covers merge into a room's furnishings by making a matching cushion for another chair or by replacing existing covered chair seats with the new material.

Net curtains   Hems of net curtains will be easier to stitch if you turn up the hem and iron it first. Instead of tacking, use hairpins to hold the hem in place for stitching.

A tear in net curtaining can be invisibly repaired with colourless nail varnish or by using egg-white as an adhesive for a patch, pressing it with a hot iron.

Nightdresses   Run narrow elastic through the hem of a nightdress to keep it away from any fire danger without restricting the wearer's movement.

Patching   An embroidery frame is useful when sewing on patches to make pinning and sewing easier. A piece of cardboard placed under the worn area is similarly helpful.

When a home-made garment needs patching, wash the patching material several times and expose it to sunlight to reduce it to the same colour as the garment.

Patch children's clothes with toy or animal shapes in contrasting colours and fabrics. Felt and corduroy are particularly suitable fabrics to use for this sort of patching.

Petticoats   For fancy dress costumes a gathered petticoat can be easily 'hooped' by threading plastic-covered curtain wire through the hem.

Pins   Keep a magnet in your workbasket to clear up fallen pins and needles after dressmaking.

A pin-cushion stuffed with steel wool will keep pins free from rust.

An elastic bracelet sewn to a pin-cushion and worn on your wrist makes pinning easier.

When sewing flimsy materials, use soap as a pin-cushion.

A small screw-top cosmetic jar makes an attractive pin-box. A piece of blotting paper kept inside it, and replaced from time to time, will prevent rusting.

Plastic raincoats   Line a clear plastic raincoat with material to match a summer dress.

Use the sleeves of an old plastic raincoat to make sleeve protectors for children to wear when they play with paints, water or sand.

Pleats   When a pleated skirt needs to be shortened, unpick the waistband and cut off the necessary length from the top of the skirt. Reduce the unwanted fullness with a row of stitching with shirring elastic and re-fit the waistband.

Pockets   Make a portable pocket in a neutral shade, with a slot or press studs which can be fastened over the belt of a pocket-less dress.

Polo-necks   For a change knit polo-neck collars separately from a sweater. Join up the sides of a straight piece of ribbed knitting of appropriate length and tuck it into or over your neckline, anchoring it with press-studs. A wool fringe could be added.

Pressing   Before sewing up the pieces of a knitted garment, roll them in a damp towel for half an hour. They can then be pressed on the reverse side without the use of a cloth.

Press-studs   When sewing on press-studs, rub chalk on the first half when it has been sewn on, then close the opening so that a chalk mark is left on the spot where the other half should be fixed.

Pulling back   To avoid dropping stitches when pulling back knitting, first thread a length of contrasting wool through the row of stitches on which knitting will re-commence.

Pyjamas   Strengthen the buttons on new pyjamas by sewing a length of tape behind the buttons and securing the buttons to it.

When children grow out of their pyjamas, turn the pyjamas into a single garment by stitching the jacket to the trouser top, thus increasing the length.

Raincoats   For extra protection against rain, stitch plastic material across the shoulders of a raincoat, between the lining and the fabric.

Scarves   When knitting a scarf, slip the first stitch of each row to produce a firm edge.

To hold a scarf in place inside a neckline, make loops with matching wool or cotton inside the collar. Curtain rings could also be used.

School caps and berets   Sew a loop of tape or elastic inside school headgear so that it will stay secure on cloakroom pegs. Also sew name tapes inside to prevent loss.

Seams   Hair-grips are handier than pins when joining the seams of knitted garments.

A seam sewn with a slightly different shade of wool makes any subsequent unpicking much easier.

When sewing up garments knitted in thick wool, a single strand of the wool will give a neater finish.

A plastic bottle gives good support inside a sleeve when sewing up the seam.

Sequins   When knitting sequins into a jumper, thread them all on the ball of wool and slip them along the wool to knit into the pattern as required.

Sewing cotton   Always cut cotton off the reel on the slant to make threading easier.

Sewing machine   After oiling a sewing machine, make sure that it is quite free from surplus oil by stitching over a sheet of blotting paper several times.

For instant measuring, glue a length of tape measure to the front of your sewing machine.

Sewing needles   An old lipstick holder makes an ideal needle-case. Press a piece of cork into the bottom to hold the needles. For your handbag, thread the needles first with an assortment of threads for emergency repairs.

When you have difficulty in threading wool, first thread the needle with a loop of cotton, then pull the wool through in the loop.

With button thread, dip the tip into nail varnish or soap, twist it and let it harden to make threading easy.

Place a cork over the end of an upholstery needle as a safety measure.

Shirring elastic is useful for shaping loosely fitting garments. Several rows of judicious shirring below a waistline will slim a skirt and a straight shapeless dress can be transformed with a shirred waistline.

Shirts   Sew another button behind the one already on the cuff so that they can be worn as link-buttons when desired.

Shoulder pads can be quickly made by cutting pieces off a foam rubber sponge.

Shoulder seams   With knitted garments, a good shoulder-line can be obtained by leaving the finished front shoulder edges on a stitch-holder until the back is finished. Then, placing right sides together, cast off in the usual way taking a stitch from both sides at the same time.

With stretch fabrics and knitwear, to prevent sagging, sew tape along the shoulder seams.

Shoulder straps Keep bra or petticoat straps out of sight by sewing a short length of tape or ribbon to the shoulder seams of dresses, fastened with a press-stud, so that underwear straps can be secured within it.

Avoid the need for buttons on a toddler's dungarees by substituting a short length of wide elastic for the cotton strap.

Keep skirt straps firmly in place by fixing press-studs at the cross-over point.

Shrinking To enable a knitted garment to be lengthened if it shrinks, knit the welts when the rest of the garment is finished, picking up the stitches from the body of the garment and working downwards. If it shrinks, it is a simple matter to increase the length of the ribbing.

A shrunken garment can be given new life with a fabric insertion at the front and a matching neckband or collar.

Skirts A strip of stiffened interlining sewn into the back hem will add fullness and style to a wide skirt.

A girl's strapless skirt will feel more secure if elastic is threaded through the back waistband.

Make a flared skirt reversible to reduce 'seating' and shine at the back by putting in zip fasteners at both sides.

If your skirt is tight at the waistline, you can obtain relief by unfastening the zip, and maintain security by hooking the hanging loop over the metal clasp on the opposite side of the opening.

To cope with the ups and downs of an everchanging waist measurement, sew several hooks and eyes on the waistband or, better still, sew lengths of self-sticking looped tape to overlap both ends of the waistband.

Repair a tear at the opening of a pleat by working an arrowhead over it and reinforcing the reverse side with a strip of iron-on carpet binding taken right across the pleat.

Sleeves Puffed sleeves can be kept shapely by stitching a length of tape from the sleeve band to the shoulder seam.

Socks Strengthen the heels and toes of home-knitted socks by knitting in sewing cotton with the wool, or by using a finer needle for these areas.

Shirring elastic knitted into the ribbing of socks will keep them firm.

To keep turn-over socks from sagging, thread elastic through the welts out of sight under the turn-over.

Soft Toys Save left-over pieces of material from dressmaking to turn into soft toys or dolls' clothes and save old nylons and net curtains for stuffing the toys or making cushions.

When stuffing a soft toy, put some pebbles in a tin or a bell inside the toy to make it more interesting, but do make sure that a child will not be able to extract them.

A narrow self-winding tape measure fastened inside a toy animal makes an amusing disappearing tail.

Stiff fabrics Soap rubbed along the seams will help a needle to penetrate thick or stiff materials when machine-stitching.

Stitch-holder When using a large safety-pin as a stitch-holder, slip a small button on first to keep the stitches away from the hinge.

A hair-grip is useful as an emergency stitch-holder.

Stocking cap Knit up odd balls of wool on four needles to a length of at least one metre, starting with a short ribbing. Add a fringe to the other end to make an attractive stocking cap.

Suede When the cuffs and pockets of a suede jacket become shabby, knit a set of matching or contrasting cuffs and pocket flaps and stitch them over the worn ones.

Tacking Use a dark thread for tacking light fabrics and a light thread for dark ones.

Keep odd lengths of embroidery silks for tacking, they will not knot as easily as ordinary sewing cotton.

With some materials, such as cotton, you can press a turned-up hem with a hot iron and avoid the need for tacking.

When tacking or gathering, thread the needle but do not break off the cotton until the needle has run the length required, when an accurate measurement can be made.

Wind tacking thread back on to a special reel so that it can be re-used.

Tape To run tape through a slot, fasten it to a large safety-pin and use this as a bodkin.

Tape measure Revive a limp tape measure by pressing it with a hot iron between waxed paper.

If you wear a sewing apron, stitch a tape measure to the hem for quick measurements.

Tea cosies When making a tea cosy, insert a sheet of plastic material between the lining and the cover to avoid staining from spills.

Towels Worn towels can be cut in half to make small guest towels or they can be strengthened by working candlewick cotton through the thinning areas. Small remnants will make face cloths.

Transfers Any design can be copied for embroidery by tracing it with a ballpoint pen and then pressing the tracing with a hot iron on the fabric. This will give you the design in reverse but, if this is not acceptable, go over the back of the tracing with a ballpoint pen and press this to the fabric.

Methylated spirits will remove transfer marks from fabric which cannot be washed.

Trousers   Protect the inside of trouser turn-ups by stitching a small button inside the back edge at the crease or by pressing a short length of self-adhesive carpet binding to the back inside edge.

Bind the back bottom edge of jeans with a strip of leather to prevent fraying and make them last longer.

Tweed   When mending tweed garments, use threads drawn carefully out of a seam-turning for a perfect match.

Valances   Make a bed valance by dyeing discarded net curtaining to match the other furnishings, then fold and gather it to fit the bed, stitching on tapes as required.

Waistbands   Stiffen a limp waistband with a plastic belt cut to the waist length and threaded through the band, or with petersham ribbon stitched on the inside of the waistband.

If a skirt waistband is too tight, nearly five centimetres can be gained by removing the waistband and unpicking the back darts. Replace the waistband, adding extra material if necessary, but usually the original overlap is sufficient to accommodate the new width.

A tight dress waistline can be treated similarly by separating the bodice from the skirt and letting out an equal number of darts in both pieces.

Wool   Knitted garments can be unpicked and the wool re-wound. To get rid of the crinkles, wind the wool around an ironing board or a piece of wood where it can be pressed with a hot iron over a damp cloth. Or secure the skeins of re-wound wool firmly and steam them or soak them in warm water until the wool has straightened, then hang them up to dry.

Short ends of wool can be used to stuff small soft toys.

Zip-fasteners   When inserting a zip-fastener, sew up the seam of the garment completely and press it. Tack and stitch the zip to the reverse side in the usual way, then unpick the seam as far as required and secure it.

Sellotape will hold a zip in position for stitching.

Secure an unreliable zip temporarily by sewing a large dress-hook near the top so that the tab of the zip can be hooked over it.

Furnishing and Storage

Pelmets to playpens

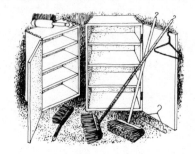

Baked limpet was our fare in the first home I ever furnished, perched on top of a granite block jutting out into the sea from the promenade.

Meal-times were variable because our kitchen and provisions in the basement were accessible by a jagged crevice only when the tide was out. Lurking rock-lice were another hazard, ever ready to send us five-year-olds tumbling back to the sandy beach if a groping hand accidentally touched one as we clambered upwards, bearing our sun-baked delicacies.

Our play-room at the highest point of the rock appeared to have been carved out of the flat surface by some giant hand, with the special needs of young humans in mind, in the shape of a small room with a table and corner seats.

This furniture may have been immovable but its uses were manifold. When we wearied of housekeeping, the rock became a fortress which no enemy could ever take or, when the tide rose high, we pirated the ocean with a fleet of paper ships.

In that make-believe world, we learned to make good use of space, each having his own rocky nook furnished with shells, driftwood and flotsam treasures in a distinctive way and in the mood of the moment.

A cursory glance at the box-planned house of the speculative builder suggests little scope for individual treatment by the home-makers of today, just as the crammed back-to-back houses of distant yesterdays leave us with the same thought. And it is accentuated by the furniture and fabric displays in the High Street which make us feel at home in any town in the kingdom.

Yet no two houses are alike. The opportunities for pursuing originality and impressing one's personality on a place of one's own are legion, whether it is a bed-sit, a mansion, a back-to-back or a rocky cave. And each brings a similar challenge and satisfaction.

The first time our young daughter decided to rearrange her bedroom by herself, we marvelled at how her enthusiasm had given her the strength to move a heavy dressing-table across the room. Thereafter, the variations were endless and we never quite knew where to find her when looking into the darkened room to tuck her up for the night.

I have no doubt that if I ever return to that rocky home on the beach, which from beginning to end of summer holidays served us so well, it will be furnished as ever with shells, seaweed and driftwood but with no resemblance to the way we had it all those years ago.

Baby basket   Bathing your baby is easier if all the bath-time necessities are stored in one place. A simple hold-all can be made by stitching rows of pockets across a length of plastic material and fitting it to a clothes-horse.

A wire filing tray, a shopping basket, a tomato box or similar containers covered with cotton or plastic make useful toilet baskets if fitted with pockets for soap, powder, safety-pins and so on.

Bags   A butcher's hook or a large cup-hook screwed inside a cupboard can be utilized to hold paper and plastic bags for ready use.

Bath mats   A loose cover of towelling will disguise a worn cork mat.

Bathroom curtains   A pair of bright towels are ideal for bathroom curtains – they are quickly made and easy to launder.

Bedroom fireplace   An unused bedroom fireplace can be pulled out and the space fitted to hold shoes or books.

Bedroom sharing   A bedroom can be divided into two by fixing curtain track to the ceiling, or the wardrobe and chests of drawers can be set at right angles to the wall and the backs fitted with pegboard for the children's pin-ups.

Bedroom stool   Convert a wooden box with a lid into a bedroom stool and linen box. Fit hinges, pad the lid with foam rubber and make a frilled cover. A piano stool is also easily convertible to bedroom use.

Beds   For increased sleeping accommodation for children in an emergency, push a double bed lengthways against a wall and turn the width of the bed into the 'length' by putting the pillows along the wall.

One sheet folded in half lengthways is often sufficient to make both top and bottom sheet for a small child's bed.

Mark the centre of blankets with coloured wool to save time when bed-making.

In very cold weather, place the eiderdown between the blankets for extra warmth.

Nylon fur fabric makes a warm and attractive bedspread.

A slip-over cover of cretonne, candlewick or quilted nylon will give a new look to a bed-head.

Beer cans   Small empty beer cans can be used to make bases for lamps.

Blankets   To deter moths, encase blankets in newspaper when storing them or scatter slices of soap among the folds of the blankets.

Lengthen a short blanket with sheeting so that it can be tucked in firmly.

Bolster cases are easier to fit if both ends are opened so that the bolster can be pulled through.

Square bolsters look attractive on a bedsitter divan instead of cushions or pillows. Cut out four sides and two end-pieces in strong fabric and strengthen the ends with a square of thick cardboard.

Book-ends   Keep book-ends in place by fixing a length of cardboard or foam rubber to the base of each book-end, facing inwards and passing underneath the books.

Brooms and brushes   Hang brushes with loops made from pipe-cleaners, instead of string, so that you can hook them on and off quickly.

Do not stand brooms on their bristles when you put them away. Screw a hook into the end of the handle or fix two cotton reels to the wall to hold the broomhead.

Buttoned upholstery   Secure a loose button with a hairpin pressed into the upholstery.

Cereal boxes, cut to shape and covered with wallpaper or self-adhesive plastic, can be fixed to the inside of cupboard doors to hold bags, greaseproof paper, jam-pot covers, doyleys and similar lightweight necessities.

Chair arms   Upholstered chair arms can be protected, or worn ones disguised, with a triangle of fabric cut to the length of the arm with the base gathered into a tassel at the front.

Cosmetic drawer   Tack elastic to the sides of a dressing table drawer, making loops of appropriate size to hold your cream jars and perfume bottles.

Cot   When your toddler's cot is no longer needed, the two long sides can be hinged together to make a clothes-horse. The short ends can be used as a gate to restrict your child's wanderings, or used to bar a window for his safety.

Cupboards   A drawing-pin stuck into the edge of a loose cupboard door will keep it closed.

Store items likely to be affected by a damp atmosphere or condensation in screwtop jars.

Curtains   Use a pipe-cleaner underneath a ribbon or cord which holds back draped curtains so that it will bear the strain for the decorative tie.

To protect a curtain facing a continually opened window, tack a spare piece of the material to the top of the curtain to bear the brunt of the dust and so lengthen the life of the curtain itself.

If you use floral instead of plain material for lining curtains, they will look more attractive from the outside and can be reversed sometimes for a fresh look inside.

When curtains have shrunk slightly, slip a curtain ring into each ring on the rail before attaching the hooks, to give a little extra length. If there is a pelmet, lengthening material can be joined to the top of the curtain where it will be hidden from view.

A wide fringe will also extend the length of a shrunken curtain or a band of plain material could be inserted into the curtains.

Curtains with a horizontal stripe or pattern will make a narrow room look wider.

To make a window appear bigger than it is, extend the curtain rails well beyond the window frame on both sides so that the entire window is exposed when the curtains are drawn back.

As an anti-draught measure, put pebbles inside the hem of floor-length curtains.

Smear curtain hooks and rails with Vaseline or petroleum jelly occasionally to keep the hooks running freely.

Cushions   When making cushion covers, cut out three pieces of the fabric to the cushion size and use one piece to make a large pocket on one side for magazines or knitting.

Shredded nylons make a soft filling for cushions.

Save large plastic bags to protect cushions which are taken into the garden.

Deck-chairs   Re-cover a deck-chair on the roller-towel principle with a double length of canvas.

Fit an extra bar of wood across the front of a deckchair, just behind the existing one, to give more support. Felt or foam rubber fitted to the front and back bars will give extra comfort and create less wear on the canvas.

Door curtain   To make a door curtain rise when the door is opened, screw a ring-hook to the top centre of the door frame and another ring near the top of the door. Tie a length of picture cord to the hook on the frame, pass it through the hook on the door and fasten it to the curtain on the opening side about 60 cm above the floor.

Door storage   Shelves fitted on the back of cloakroom doors can be used for shoes, tools, cleaning equipment and so on. Narrow shelves on pantry doors are similarly useful.

Drawers   Discarded long drawers will convert into cupboards or bookcases, standing upright with shelves and doors added.

Dressing tables   When space is limited, fix a long mirror and a shelf to a cupboard or wardrobe door to serve as a dressing table.

Duvets   When making duvet covers, economize on material by using a redundant sheet for the underside.

A length of sheeting sewn to the bottom of a duvet cover can be tucked under the mattress to anchor the duvet securely in cold weather.

Fireplace   Brighten an empty fireplace in summertime by filling the gap with trellis or peg-board and trailing plants. A poster glued to hardboard is an alternative.

Footstool   Make a footstool from four or five thick telephone directories by putting them into an old cushion cover and fastening them securely together. Then make a close-fitting cover in moquette for it.

Gloves   Make a holder for gloves, scarves and headgear on the shoe-bag principle with a row of pockets for each member of the family, to save time and prevent losses.

Halls   Narrow halls will appear more spacious if decorated in light colours. Mirrors open out enclosed areas too. Place them to face the front door and opposite doors leading off the hall.

A hall window can be turned into a striking decorative feature by the addition of glass shelves fitted right across the window to hold trailing plants, coloured glassware or other attractive objects.

Fit a narrow shelf over a hall doorway to display ornaments.

Kitchens   In a small house, you can ease kitchen congestion by removing the kitchen or pantry door and hanging plastic strip curtaining across the opening. Reversing a door to make it open into the hall is an alternative remedy for lack of space.

Half-shelves fitted into a kitchen cupboard will hold small items. A cutlery box standing on its side is similarly useful.

A kitchen-drawer handle can be replaced with a towel rail.

Lampshades   Coloured holiday snapshots glued to a plain lampshade can look attractive when the light is switched on. Postage stamps, maps, dried flowers and toy or animal shapes can all be used in this way.

Loft   Keep a list pinned inside the loft door as a reminder of things deposited in the loft.

Magazines   A tray fixed to the leg supports of an occasional table is useful for holding magazines.

Moths   Place pieces of dried orange peel, cloves or shredded soap between stored garments and blankets to deter moths and keep the articles fresh.

Clothing sealed in a plastic bag will also be safe from moths.

Pantry shelf   A wire office-tray fixed to a pantry wall will make an airy holder for butter, cheese and similar items.

Plastic peg-baskets fixed to a rod under a pantry shelf are useful for holding fruit and vegetables.

Pelmets For easy removal and replacement, fix fabric pelmets to their board with carpet press-studs or self-sticking looped tape.

Pictures Protect pictures from dampness by fitting aluminium foil to the back of the frame.

Protect the wall from picture marks by fixing drawing pins or a cork to the back of the frame, thus allowing the air to circulate.

A strip of self-adhesive foam rubber fixed on the back lower edge of a picture frame will keep it steady.

In a child's bedroom, an area of wall covered with polystyrene or cork tiles will look attractive and allow him to pin up a succession of pictures without spoiling the wallpaper with pinholes.

Disused picture frames can be backed and painted to make trays.

Plaque supports Stand a plaque or decorative plate on a small rubber band to prevent it from slipping on polished surfaces.

A grooved rubber soap-saver cut into strips will also hold plates securely on a polished surface.

Plate storage Prevent damage to plates when stacking them by placing a paper tissue or a bottling ring between each one.

Playpen If a playpen takes up too much room, reduce it to triangular size and put it in the corner of a room.

A discarded playpen can be dismantled and the sides used to make gates for stairs and doorways or bars for windows, as protection for toddlers.

Pram basket A disused wicker pram basket can be used as a magazine rack, a holder for trailing plants, or it could be fitted to a kitchen or hall cupboard wall and used to hold fruit and vegetables, gloves and scarves or cleaning equipment.

Pram mattress A plastic cover for a pram mattress in the shape of a pillow-case will stay in position better than a loose piece of waterproof fabric.

Rugs Keep rugs anchored on a polished floor by sewing rubber bottling rings to the corners and along the sides.

When heavy chair legs have flattened the fibres of a rug, cover the area with a dampened cloth and place a hot iron briefly on it, or use a steam iron. Raise the fibres with a strong comb, working against the carpet pile.

Hooks screwed to the floor near the hearth will hold a rug in position with curtain rings sewn underneath its edge at appropriate intervals.

Coat the back of a limp rug with a strong size solution or with shellac to restore its original stiffness.

The end pieces of a rug worn threadbare in the middle can be salvaged to make slip mats.

Safety net A pram safety net will double as a safety gate when fastened to four hooks fixed to door jambs or to the foot of the stairs.

Scarves Fix a length of expanding curtain wire inside a hall cupboard or a wardrobe to hold scarves uncreased.

Screwtop jars The lids of screwtop jars can be painted to form a set of storage jars.

Fasten screwtop jars by their lids to the underside of pantry or workshop shelves for extra storage space.

Sheets Save time searching for the right-sized sheet by creating your own identification system on the hem, with stitching in different colours or simply by marking each corner S or D.

Shelves When turning out a cupboard, line the shelves with several layers of paper so that when the top layer is grubby it can be withdrawn easily leaving a clean sheet.

Blotting paper will absorb dampness and drips on pantry or kitchen shelves.

A set of shelves can be used to divide a large room.

Shoe trees Make a perfectly fitting shoe tree by pushing some dampened newspaper tightly into the front of the shoe. When it has dried, it can be used regularly to keep the shoes in shape.

A length of pliable wood, such as a ruler, with a wad of cotton wool or tissue paper will substitute for a shoe tree.

Skirts Two clothes pegs fastened to a coat-hanger will hold skirts in shape or, alternatively, screw two small hooks to a wooden coat-hanger to hold the skirt loops.

Sliding door Lessen the banging when closing a sliding door by fixing rubber-headed tacks to the jamb to act as bumpers.

Soap Store tablets of soap and bars of household soap, preferably cut to tablet size, in a warm place to harden them and make them last longer.

A large glass jar filled with a variety of coloured soaps or cotton-wool balls makes an attractive bathroom decoration.

Stairs Wrap stair pads in newspapers for added thickness and to deter moths.

65

Always make sure that your stair carpet is well tacked down to prevent accidents which can happen if carpeting is loose.

When you buy stair carpet, add an extra half-metre to the length so that you can alter the position of the carpet from time to time to vary the tread and make it last longer.

Colour threadbare patches on stair carpet by painting them with a strong solution of dye of the appropriate colour.

Make extra space in a cupboard beneath the stairs by fixing shelf brackets to the stair risers.

To have easy access to items stored in a small cupboard under the stairs, make a set of shelves on castors which can be pulled out when something is required.

Stow-aways Screw castors to disused drawers and use them for under-bed storage.

When using large cardboard boxes for storage, choose boxes of the same size. Line them up under a bedroom window or on the landing and conceal them under a flounced cretonne cover.

Table mats Revive shabby table mats by making pockets of gingham or other material into which they can be slipped and easily withdrawn for washing.

Off-cuts of floor coverings can also be shaped to size and covered to make table mats.

Cork tiles also make attractive table mats.

Sandwich a piece of foam rubber between two plastic doyleys and stitch or crochet them together to make a washable table mat.

An attractive handbag can be made by crocheting two straw table mats together and attaching handles or by inserting sides with two strips of canvas and adding handles.

Teapot stands Ceramic tiles make attractive and functional teapot stands. Glue cork or felt underneath to protect surfaces from scratches.

Tidiness A chest with a personal drawer for each member of the family is invaluable in the kitchen or utility room. Items left lying about can be swiftly returned to the owner's drawer.

Plastic buckets and wastepaper bins make ideal toy boxes.

Hooks fixed at a low level in a clothes cupboard encourage children to be tidy.

Fix castors under toy boxes and heavy toys such as dolls' houses and forts to make them easy to handle.

Make a set of pockets in strong fabric to hold dolls and soft toys. Rings or a coat-hanger can be fastened to it for hanging it up.

Encourage children to tidy up their playthings quickly with a game of 'beat the egg-timer' or 'beat the clock'.

Ties   Fix a towel rail inside a wardrobe to hold ties.

Trays standing on the floor can be kept under control with a length of curtain wire fixed to the wall.

Umbrellas   A row of spring-clip tool-holders fixed to a cloakroom wall will hold umbrellas.

Vases   Marbles look attractive inside glass vases and will act as a support for the flower stems.

Velvet   Roll velvet curtains around a broom handle or thickly rolled newspaper when storing them, to avoid fold marks.

Wastepaper bins can be made from large food tins or beer cans covered with fabric, self-adhesive plastic or wallpaper.

General Maintenance
Cars to castors

One of my pastimes as a six-year-old was to watch a family friend making tomato boxes. Soon I found that if I stood long enough in silent admiration and envy he would give me a hammer and nails so that I too could contribute to the export trade.

My son must have inherited this passion for the hammer because by the age of four, he could drive home as straight a nail as any craftsman. No birthday present gave him greater joy than a pound of two-inch ovals, a claw hammer and a block of wood.

At some stage between my first tomato box and my son's heavily nailed block of wood, I used carpet tacks to fasten a date box to the back of a cupboard door under the kitchen sink. This was in our first home, the tiniest of flats, high amid city roof-tops. Space, like furniture coupons and my husband's visits in those wartime days, was at a premium and I desperately needed a shelf for my soap powder.

Later I was to learn about brackets, centre punches and screws with counter-sunk heads. In due course we were proud possessors of an electric drill, spoon bits and a variety of saws, but no subsequent job, using all this sophisticated ironmongery, produced half as much satisfaction as that crude date-box shelf.

In spite of possessing all the right tools, however, some ostensibly straightforward job can suddenly present an almost insuperable problem, often when it is too late to turn back.

Our spare bedroom had a fireplace, unused for many years. It was of the one-piece metal variety, married to the brickwork of the chimney breast by two screws. Its simple removal, my husband claimed, would provide space for book-shelves and a shoe-rack.

He took out the holding screws and, with a determined tug, he parted the fireplace from the chimney breast in a cloud of soot and plaster, leaving a black gaping hole.

Nowadays, the best holes in chimney breasts boast a horizontal concrete lintel to hold up the brickwork on its way to the ceiling and beyond. But our hole had no such refinement. As brick after brick dislodged itself and dropped to the sooty hearth, the black gaping hole grew and grew.

Saving the rest of that chimney breast was a lengthy and nerve-racking experience. Our garden fence was never the same after great lengths of it were dragged upstairs for a frantic, temporary shoring-up process.

I am no advocate of 'If at first you don't succeed, call in the builder/joiner/plumber', but I set great store by 'But what if . . .?', a phrase my husband always mutters these days before embarking on the unknown.

This way many a disintegrating chimney breast could be saved and, come to that, maybe chimney stacks and chimney pots as well.

Acrylic ware   Remove a scratch on an acrylic bath by rubbing it with fine sandpaper and restoring the shine with metal polish.

Brickwork   Smarten shabby brickwork or cover up paint splashes on it by rubbing them with a piece of broken brick.

Brick window sills can be brightened with red tile paint.

Lighten a room facing a brick wall by treating the wall with white emulsion paint. Small enclosed gardens will also benefit from this treatment which creates an illusion of spaciousness.

Cars   Replace a vandalized car aerial with a wire coat-hanger, straightened and cut to the required length. Force the wire into the remains of the aerial and fix a threaded nut to the free end. It may no longer retract but radio reception will be excellent. Prevent vandalism to a car aerial by smearing it with black grease. But mind your fingers when you want to adjust it!

After changing wheels to rotate the tyre position, record the interchange and mileage on the wheel or use the inside of the hub cap to record all details of the wheel's history.

To immobilize a car, remove the rotor arm in the distributor.

If you have to leave your car outside overnight in frosty weather, protect the windscreen from icing with newspaper.

If you leave your car unattended often, stick tape over the serial number of the ignition key, on the dashboard, to deter thieves.

A spare key taped securely to some hidden part of the bodywork may rejoice your heart one day.

A small dent in a car body can be pulled out with a rubber suction cap and by applying a hot cloth or a hot water bottle to the back of the dent until it springs back into shape.

Keep distilled water in a well-rinsed polythene squirter-bottle for easy application.

Keep the garage floor free from oil by positioning a shallow tin of sand under a car to catch drips from the engine. Replace the sand regularly. The discarded oily sand is useful for starting a bonfire.

Hang up an old tyre at the end of the garage for guidance and protection when driving in. If you fix old plastic hosepipe or lengths of any discarded rubber items to the garage walls, they will protect car doors when opened carelessly.

A table-tennis ball suspended appropriately from the roof will help you to position the car as you drive into the garage.

A ladder laid down the centre of the garage floor will also act as a guide, but make sure that the ladder is clear of projections on the underside of the car, and be careful.

In winter keep some pieces of mineralized roofing felt or discarded raincoats in the boot to slip under the wheels in case you ever get stuck in the snow.

A long-handled mop carried in the car will allow you to de-mist the back window from the front seat, but don't try this while you're driving.

Protect chromium by washing off road-salt regularly in the winter months and by coating the chromium fittings with a thin film of petroleum jelly, Vaseline or wax polish.

Carpets   If you find moth larvae in a carpet, brush and vacuum clean the area, then press it with a very hot iron over a damp cloth several times.

Try colouring worn or moth-eaten patches of carpet with a felt-tipped pen.

Use a carpet-sweeper or a hand-brush instead of a vacuum cleaner on a new carpet for the first few months to ensure that any loose fibres settle down.

Old denim, cut into strips, makes a good substitute for carpet webbing for joins and binding.

Castors   If a castor's screw-hole has become enlarged, put a match-stick or some steel wool into the hole before screwing home the castor.

Chair Legs   Prevent chair legs from marking linoleum and parquet floors by sticking small pieces of felt to the leg ends.

Chimneys   If a chimney catches fire, quickly close all your doors and windows and throw salt on the fire.

China   When mending china, keep the pieces in position after cementing by fixing lumps of plasticine or strips of Sellotape under the joins.

Chromium nuts   To prevent damage to a chromium-plated nut when tightening or loosening it, cover the nut with adhesive plaster.

Cigarette burns   Rubbing the burnt fibres with sandpaper will remove slight burn marks from carpets and rugs.

Coal bricks   Turn coal dust into coal bricks by mixing together eight parts of coal dust with one part of cement. Gradually add water until the mixture is stiff, fill flower pots with it and turn them out when set.

Alternatively, simply save cardboard packets and egg boxes and fill them with coal dust.

Coal effect fires   Revive fading artificial coal on an electric fire with black gloss paint or black shoe polish.

Coal saver   Keep an ordinary builder's brick at the back of the fire-basket and build the fire over it. As a result, you will have a bigger fire and the brick will retain some heat when the fire goes out.

Coal shovel   Paint the handle of a coal shovel white to make it easier to find in the dark.

Concrete   When mixing concrete, add one tablespoonful of soapless detergent to each bucket of cement to make it easier to mix and stronger.

Decorating quantities   After decorating, keep a pencilled record (in some unseen corner of the room, or on the top of the door) of the quantities of paint and wallpaper used and the date of application.

Door banging   Hang a pad of plastic foam around the leading edge of the door frame, from handle to handle, to stop a door banging when it has to be kept open. This system can also be used to prevent toddlers locking themselves in rooms.

Doorbells   If the sound of a doorbell is too harsh, stick a piece of adhesive plaster on the spot where the clapper strikes.

Door hanging   When screwing the hinges in position, use a large wooden wedge to support the door. If a door is too wide for the frame, plane the hinged side to avoid having to re-seat the handle. Hinge seatings will, of course, require adjustment.

Door hinges   Rub squeaking door hinges with Vaseline or a pencil.

Door rattling   Doors can be made to close tightly by fixing pieces of felt or foam rubber at various points on the door frame. The most effective spot is usually near the handle.

Door-stop   Screwed to the floor and painted to match the decorations, a cotton reel will serve as a door-stop.
   A spring ball-catch, as used on cupboard doors, can be fixed to the floor to hold a door open.

Doorway   A disused doorway can be made attractive by fitting shelves into it and using it as a bookcase or display unit.

Drain-pipes which spoil the appearance of a garden wall or an entrance can be camouflaged with trellis. This can be painted and hung with pot plants if desired. '

Draught excluder   A strip of wood fixed across the floor to fit closely to the outside of a door will exclude draught. This can be made even more effective by sticking plastic foam or felt along its edge or by tacking the edge of a slip mat to it.
   A long tube of stout fabric filled with sand will mould itself to uneven

gaps beneath a door. For outer doors through which the rain beats, cover the 'sausage' with plastic material.

Drawers can be made to run in and out smoothly by rubbing the runners with candlegrease, bar soap, talcum powder or lead pencil.

Dustbin If your dustbin is likely to be overturned by wind or scavenging animals, drive a stake into the ground and loop the handle over it.

Inner tubing from a bicycle or car wheel, fitted to the rim of a dustbin, will reduce the clatter of the lid.

Electric fan Fix a plastic foam mat to the base of an electric fan to keep it steady.

Electric flex can be quickly stripped of its insulation by removing the outer cotton or plastic covering and burning away the rubber or plastic insulation covering each core, leaving the requisite length of bared copper wire.

Electric fires Get the maximum benefit from the reflector by keeping it dust-free and polished regularly with metal polish, unplugging the fire first, of course.

Electric fuses Keep a spare fuse-holder wired, ready to replace a fused one.

It is helpful to have each fuse labelled to show which points it serves.

Electric light bulbs To remove a bulb which has broken in its socket, turn off the current at the mains supply and push a cork into the base of the broken bulb. Twist to remove it.

Electric shaver Get a firm grip on an electric shaver by winding several rubber bands around it.

Electric sockets With children in the house, all electric sockets should be of the switch-and-shutter type. If they are not, cover the outlet with adhesive tape or, safer still, keep a blank plug handy for blocking the socket when it is not in use. Special plugs can also be bought for this purpose.

Enamel Protect all enamel-surfaced kitchen equipment with regular applications of silicone wax polish.

End grain Smooth off the rough end of a piece of wood with a smearing of plaster of paris before painting or staining.

Fire-lighters A large cinder soaked overnight in paraffin, in a large paint tin kept for this purpose, will make an excellent fire-lighter, set on crumpled newspaper.

Fold old sheets of newspaper into tight strips, then form them into a ring and use five or six of these to light a fire without firewood. Coke boilers can be lit this way too but more newspaper rings will be needed.

Soak old newspaper in water until pulped, then squeeze it into hard balls and dry them in a warm place. They take up little storage space and provide instant fire-lighters.

Dissolve candle ends and dip folded newspaper in the wax for fire-lighting.

A difficult fire will sometimes respond to a flaming ball of newspaper placed on top of it.

A fire will keep in most of the night if the ashes from beneath the fire-basket are shovelled on top of the coals so that they are completely covered.

Fire prevention Always close living-room and kitchen doors at night to minimize any possible fire damage.

Always disconnect radio, television and other electrical equipment plugs from their sockets overnight or when leaving the house for a period.

Floors Gaps in floorboards cause draughts but these can be eliminated in many ways, according to their size. Strips of thin wood can be tapped in until flush with the floor; a paste of shellac and sawdust can be pressed in; papiermâché made from pulped newspaper and flour paste or glue will dry hard enough to sandpaper; putty or plastic wood can be used or coarse string can be forced into narrow gaps.

When you have taken up floorboards for electrical or plumbing purposes, fasten them back with screws instead of nails to make any subsequent removal easier.

When a floor has been soaked by rain or a leakage, fill all available hot water bottles, kettles and saucepans with hot water and place them between the boards and the floor covering.

Freeze-ups Lumps of salt distributed at night in the kitchen and bathroom will prevent the sink and bath outlets and the lavatory pan from freezing in icy weather.

Guard against falls on icy doorsteps and footpaths by keeping them sprinkled with salt.

Gas pipes Bubble-blowing solution brushed on a suspected gas leak will form a bubble if there is a leak.

As a temporary measure, until the gas fitter arrives, cover a gas leak with softened soap and bind it liberally with strips of bandaging.

If you know where the gas pipes and electric cables run beneath the floorboards, mark their position for future tenants or to refresh your own memory.

Glass   After a breakage, mop up glass splinters with a dampened paper tissue which can be thrown away. Then run the vacuum cleaner over the surrounding area to make sure that no pieces of glass remain.

Glazing   Before applying putty, paint the window frame to prevent the wood absorbing oil from the putty. Help the putty to adhere by scoring the wood in places.

Gravel   Strengthen a gravel drive by raking a thin sand and cement mixture into it.

Hammers   Tighten a loose hammer-head by soaking it in oil or water.

To remove the broken end of a hammer handle, put the hammer-head in a fire until the wood in the socket has burnt out.

Protect the heads of upholstery tacks by covering the hammer-head with adhesive plaster or wide rubber bands.

Handbasin crack   Paint over a crack in a handbasin on the underside, stick a strip of muslin over it, then apply paint again several times.

Handles   Loose handles can be secured by forcing a thin sliver of wood into the hole with the handle.

Hardboard   When sawing hardboard, cover the guide-line with Sellotape and saw through it to avoid a splintered edge.

High chair   Before you throw out a wooden high chair, consider the possibility of converting part of it into a stool, a desk or a swing seat. If you must throw it out give it to a local café or restaurant where it will be extremely useful for mothers with toddlers eating there.

Holes   When making a hole in plaster, drill through a piece of Sellotape or aluminium foil placed over the spot to prevent the plaster from cracking. With an enamel surface, stick a piece of brown paper over the spot first.

Hooks   Slip a wooden clothes peg over a cup-hook when screwing it in or out to act as a lever.

Hosepipes   To store hosepipes, wind them around a bucket, an old wastepaper basket or a tyre-less car wheel fastened to a wall.

Plastic hosepipes are easier to coil when warm, so let the hot water tap run through them for a few seconds after use.

If a hosepipe nozzle is too loose for a tap, wind rubber bands around the tap until the hosepipe grips.

Instructions   Keep all the instructions and guarantees for your household appliances in one large envelope for easy reference.

Kettles   Replace a broken knob on a kettle lid with a cork, screwing it on from inside the lid.

Linoleum and vinyl floor covering will be easier to handle if it is opened out and left in a warm room for several hours before laying.

When replacing floor coverings, use the old piece as a pattern.

To hold any rising dampness in check lay roofing felt beneath linoleum on a concrete floor.

After laying, linoleum is usually left to stretch for several weeks before the final trimming. During this period, cover the overlapping edges with Sellotape to protect them.

Fix quadrant beading around a room after laying linoleum, to exclude draughts from the skirting-boards.

To patch linoleum, cut out the worn piece with a sharp knife and use it as a pattern for the new piece which should be fixed with a strong glue.

Worn linoleum can be stippled with a contrasting colour of linoleum paint, dabbed on with a sponge.

Use pieces of linoleum and other floor coverings to make protective wall panels behind a cooker or beside a door.

Locks   To lubricate a lock, dip the key in oil or in powdered lead pencil.

Make a mortise lock burglar-proof by fixing a retaining-hook alongside the lock, so that the hook will slip into the eye of the key, when the door is locked, and grip it firmly. It will then be impossible to interfere with the key from the outside or insert a duplicate key in the lock.

To prevent the removal of counter-sunk wood screws in locks, before inserting the screw, file away the upper right and lower left corners of the screw-head slot, viewing it horizontally. Thus, any screwdriver attempting to remove the screw will be unable to get sufficient grip to turn it.

Meters   Searching for the gas or electric meter slot in the dark will be easier if you paint it with luminous paint. Always leave a coin in the slot ready to be pushed in.

Nails   To keep nails steady when you hammer them, grip them with pliers or wedge them between the teeth of an old comb, or stick them through a piece of card.

Keep nails of various sizes in screwtop jars, screwing the lids to the underside of a shelf to save space. Drop a little oil into each jar to prevent rusting.

When withdrawing nails from painted woodwork, hold a paint-stripping blade beneath the pliers to prevent damage to the woodwork.

Nuts and bolts To prevent rusting and to make any subsequent removal easy, dip the thread of a bolt in shellac or clear polyurethane varnish.

Oil Old motor oil can be used as a substitute for creosote on fences.

Extend the spout of an oilcan to reach awkward places with a length of wire, a drinking straw or plastic tubing.

An empty nail varnish bottle with a brush can be used to apply oil.

Painting Stand an unopened tin of paint upside down the day before you use it so that it will be easier to mix. Placing it in a warm room also helps.

You can ascertain the dry colour of a paint by brushing a small amount on a piece of white blotting paper.

When painting chairs or tables, stand the legs in a tin lid or drive nails into the end of each leg.

Remove the door fittings, if possible, when painting a door. Alternatively, protect the metal with Sellotape or masking tape.

When staining floors, hold a sheet of metal or cardboard against the skirting-board to protect it from splashes.

Cover a paint-roller tray with aluminium foil or put it inside a strong plastic bag to reduce cleaning time.

A foam rubber hair-curler pushed on the handle of a paint brush will catch the drips as you paint. For large brushes, wind a strip of towelling around the handle several times to form a wide absorbent ring.

Half a rubber ball, a paper plate or an aluminium foil baking case can also be used on a brush to catch drips from overhead painting.

When working outside in the sunshine, prevent a skin forming on the paint by covering the tin with aluminium foil, allowing a gap for the brush.

Flies and insects will avoid paint to which a few drops of oil of wintergreen or citronella have been added.

Soak new brushes before use in water or, preferably, boiled linseed oil, brushing it off and drying them afterwards, of course.

It pays to develop a reliable system of squeezing off excess paint when you load your brush. Wire or string can be fixed across tins which have handles. A segment can be cut out of a tin lid, making a lid to fit each standard size of paint tin and retained for repeated usage.

A nail driven through the handle of a large paint brush close to and parallel with the bristle head, will support the brush on the rim of the tin. A tack or cup-hook will support a smaller brush.

Several nails hammered into the top of a step-ladder around a paint tin will keep it secure or it can be placed in an old round cake tin, screwed to the ladder top.

Stick brown paper tape, Sellotape or masking tape around window frames to keep the edge of the glass clean. Or protect the entire window by pasting newspaper over the glass or by smearing it with softened soap.

Bind the bristles with a rubber band when painting window-frames or similar woodwork which requires a neat edge.

A razor blade will ease off paint around the edges of the pane and a coin or steel wool will rub off splashes.

A paint brush required later for the same colour can be left standing in water. When needed, brush off all the water on newspaper or rag.

If you have to leave your painting hurriedly, wrap the brush tightly in aluminium foil until it can be cleaned.

Soak brushes in paraffin or turpentine to clean off all the paint, bending a piece of wire to fit across the top of the tin to suspend them in the cleaning solution, enabling dissolving paint to drain. An old comb will help to clean out the bristles. Finally, wash them in hot soapy water and ammonia. Rinse and dry.

Cleaning liquid for paint brushes can be used repeatedly if the sediment is allowed to settle and the clear liquid poured off.

Screw a small cup-hook into the handles of paint brushes and hang them on the bar of a wire coat-hanger for space-saving storage.

Clean the rim of a paint tin before replacing the lid to ensure a good seal. A round of aluminium foil placed on top of the remaining paint will prevent a skin forming.

Mark on the outside the level of paint remaining in a tin. Small quantities of surplus paint are best stored in screwtop jars for easy identification.

Store a partly-used paint tin upside down. When opening it again, pour the paint immediately into another tin before stirring it so that any skin which has formed is left in the original tin.

Paint with loose skin in it should be strained through a nylon stocking into a clean tin. Instead of throwing away the paint skin, use it to strengthen thinning metal in articles such as buckets and coal scuttles. Paste it on with a pad of newspaper or rag and leave it to harden.

Paraffin, white spirit or turpentine will remove fresh paint spots from clothing. A piece of the same fabric will often remove fresh paint spots. For example, rub tweed carefully with tweed.

Paint spots on shoes should be gently rubbed with steel wool and shoe polish.

A matchstick, dipped in paint and left to dry, is handy when you want to look for toning curtains or wallpaper.

Planes   Rub a plane with candlegrease to make it run smoothly.

Pointing   When pointing brickwork, apply the cement mixture through a slot cut in a sheet of metal bent to form a tray to hold the mixture, so that any surplus is readily retrieved for re-use.

Polystyrene   Use a heated knife to cut polystyrene.

Putty   A small V-shaped pulley is useful for cutting strips of putty for glazing.

A hot poker rubbed carefully over old putty will ease it out of a window-frame. Paint stripper also helps to remove old putty.

Putty will stay pliable if stored in a plastic bag or if wrapped tightly in aluminium foil. It will also remain soft if stored in a jar of water.

Radiator   Line the wall behind a radiator with aluminium foil to reflect the heat into the room.

Roof tiles   After removing a green growth from roof tiles, swill the tiles well and give them two or three coatings of waterglass to prevent a re-infestation.

Sandpaper   Increase the life of a sanding disc by tapping it, when rotating, with a wire brush to clear the dust.

Make a sandpaper block by fastening a strip of sandpaper to the lid of a flat tin with the ends fastened inside. A piece of handrail with a flat base also makes an ideal block.

Grooved surfaces can be sandpapered more easily if the sandpaper is wrapped around a foam rubber sponge or a lump of putty. Making slits in a sheet of sandpaper also helps when working on mouldings.

Scissors   Sharpen scissors with a cutting motion on the neck of a bottle. Kitchen scissors can be sharpened by cutting sandpaper into strips.

Screws   When driving a screw into an awkward position, push it through a piece of cardboard so that it can be easily held in place.

Cycle valve tubing can help with the handling of small screws. Slip the head of a small screwdriver into the tubing, leaving just enough space to take the head of the screw as well when you drive it in.

A rusty screw can be loosened for withdrawal by holding a hot poker to its head before using the screwdriver.

Tighten a loose screw by wrapping some steel wool around it before driving it in, or dip the screw in French polish or knotting for the same effect.

Screws will be easier to drive in if you rub them first with grease, soap, beeswax, paraffin or graphite.

Turn an old tray into a screw-carrier by fixing a handle in the centre and screwing tins to the tray to hold a selection of screws, nails, tacks and other items.

You may be able to loosen the rust on an obstinate screw with a hammer blow.

A few drops of paraffin left soaking into the wood surrounding a screw will sometimes help to ease it out.

A screwdriver holder can be simply made by boring holes of varying sizes in a length of wood and fastening this wood to the wall to make a shelf.

To prevent rusting, keep screws and nails in an old Vaseline or petroleum jelly jar.

Sediment To strain sediment from bottles of turpentine, paint solvent and similar liquids, pack the neck of the bottle with steel wool and pour the liquid through it.

Small parts When dismantling fittings, radios, record players and similar items, use a ridged car mat to keep the screws and nuts under control as they are removed. A strip of Sellotape will keep very small screws safe.

Snow When clearing snow, coat the spade with glycerine to prevent snow from sticking to it.

When snow seeps through the rafters and blisters a ceiling, prick the bubble of water with a darning needle and let the water drip through slowly. Finally, press the paper flat with a soft cloth.

Soldering Clean a soldering iron before use by wiping it, when heated, over a pad of steel wool.

Make a holder for items to be soldered by fixing two spring-type clothes pegs to a bevelled edge of a block of wood.

Spanner When a spanner is too big, hold a screwdriver beside the nut to fill up the gap.

Springs To secure a loose spring in an arm-chair, staple a strong suspender, cut to the appropriate length, to the woodwork and clip it on the spring.

Steel drilling To maintain a constant supply of oil when drilling holes in steel plate, make a ring of putty around the hole to hold the oil.

Step-ladders Screw cup-hooks on both sides at the top of a step-ladder to hold tins of paint or other equipment.

Fix an old baking tin to the top step to hold nails, tools, buckets and so on in safety.

A holder for tools can be made on the top of a step-ladder with a length of expanding curtain wire, secured at intervals to provide a grip.

Make the treads of a step-ladder slip-proof by painting them and sprinkling sand over the wet paint. The ladder itself can be made slip-proof by tacking foam rubber or pieces of an old hot water bottle to its feet.

Stone steps A worn stone door-step can often be reversed to give a flat surface on top. Pack the worn side underneath with cement.

String-holder Fasten a plastic funnel to a kitchen or workshop wall to hold a ball of string with the end coming out of the spout. A disused teapot can also be used to dispense string.

Taps If you are unable to renew a faulty tap washer immediately and cannot bear the sound of dripping any longer, tie a piece of string or a strip of rag to the tap to convey the drips quietly to the plug-hole.

Unscrew a tight tap by winding a leather strap around the collar and pulling sharply in alternate directions until it loosens.

Tiles Rub new fireplace tiles with olive oil before lighting the fire for the first time to prevent any possibility of cracking the glaze.

Timber tidy Make a holder for odd lengths of timber by fastening a batten to each end of a length of wire netting. Bring the battens together and fix them to a wall on large cup-hooks.

Tools Make one side of the handle of tools flat to prevent them from rolling off a work-bench.

Fasten a strip of webbing or rubber to a shelf edge or to a wall, tacking it at intervals to hold tools.

Store your tools and garden implements over a painted outline of their shape so that you can see at a glance if you have forgotten to replace one.

Varnish Old varnish can be softened and removed with methylated spirits applied on a wad of cotton wool.

Varnish will be easier to apply if you stand the tin in hot water for an hour before using it.

Vice jaws Cement a strip of thin leather to each side of a vice to protect the wood or metal being treated.

Wallpaper When stripping wallpaper, use a long-handled mop to reach to the top of high walls for soaking them and use a garden hoe to strip the area.

Hot water with soapless detergent added soaks wallpaper quickly and a garden syringe with a fine nozzle is useful for applying it.

Slashing the surface of old wallpaper with a knife or wire brush helps the water to penetrate, but take care to avoid damaging the plaster beneath.

Soak stubborn small pieces of wallpaper with water and apply a hot iron to remove them.

When choosing a wallpaper pattern, bear in mind that an embossed design will later look attractive if painted over with emulsion paint.

Before you start hanging wallpaper, drop a plumb-line from the ceiling and mark the true vertical line on each wall for the first sheet of paper. This procedure is essential for accurate paper-hanging because, unfortunately, few walls, ceilings or corners are absolutely true.

Always work towards the door and away from a window when applying wallpaper so that the joins will be less apparent.

When fixing wallpaper, press it smooth with a roll of kitchen paper, discarding pieces as they become wet.

If your seam roller marks the paper, soften it by wrapping adhesive tape around it. A chair castor will substitute for a seam roller or you can pat the seams flat with a folded towel.

Remove a paste bubble in wallpaper by pricking it with a darning needle and carefully pressing out the surplus paste.

When patching wallpaper, tear off the old piece and tear a slightly larger piece of the same shape to match the pattern, tearing very carefully so that the patterned side of the paper slightly overlaps the pasting side. In this way, you can achieve an invisible patch.

To make horizontal joins less noticeable, tear the paper edge, instead of cutting it, and lap the lower edge over the upper one when they are above eye level, and the upper one over the lower one when they are below eye level.

When you have to cut unperforated border paper, or want to reduce its width, run it through an unthreaded sewing machine, set to the shortest stitch, to make it tear easily.

Wall plugs   In masonry, a piece of aluminium foil or steel wool can be used as a plug. Wet the steel wool so that it will rust quickly and give a firm lasting hold.

A short length of pencil will also substitute for a wall plug.

When drilling a wall, protect the skirting-board and collect the falling dust in a sheet of newspaper, one edge of which has been dipped in water so that it will cling to the wall above the skirting-board.

Wastepipes   As a protection against frost, cover the outside junction of the bathroom wastepipes with hardboard or floor covering, cut to size.

Tie a small balloon, with a slit in it, over a lavatory cistern overflow pipe to prevent icy draughts blowing through it. The slit will allow any overflowing water to escape.

Lagged outside pipes can be given extra protection by covering the lagging with plastic fabric to keep it dry.

Windows   You can increase the light from a dormer window by fixing mirrors at both sides of the window.

Odds and Ends
Cats to key-rings

The article I sigh for most when it is missing is a newspaper.

It could happen on a dank November day when windows stream with condensation, or in spring when I'm sowing sweet peas, or when I'm storing away blankets, or when the wind whistles through the floorboards, or when the dust-bin is emptied, or when shoes and sweaters need their drying speeded. In fact, on most days, although replete with news and views and recipes, I can never spare my newspaper.

Hidden depths, however, are by no means confined to newspapers.

A potato can be baked, boiled, mashed, chipped, frittered and in dozens of other ways prepared for the dining-table. But a raw slice of that same potato, strapped to a sufferer's back, has been known to relieve the agonies of lumbago, while two potatoes, peeled and placed between the sheets, proved a remarkable cure for someone afflicted for years with painful night cramp.

Many a smoker keeps his tobacco moist with a fresh slice of potato in his pouch and many a tight shoe has been loosened overnight with a slice in the offending shoe. Your kettles, your cuttings, your complexion, your chimneys and chilblains will all welcome the attention of a potato.

And, just as the potato is not only for eating, so tea is not, of necessity, always for drinking; a tooth-brush can do much more than clean your teeth; a pipe-cleaner can fulfil many a pleasanter role; and the relatively short lives of successive pairs of tights need not be lamented when you realize for how many other jobs they are fitted when their leg-work is over.

Then there are thumbs and elephants.

Once, a little Dutch boy realized that his thumb was not solely for sucking. He diverted it as a temporary plug for a hole in a dyke and thus achieved a lasting place in the hall of fame.

There was a similar incident, but of vaster proportions, in India when a canal bank sprang a leak and put ripening crops in danger. An elephant-riding passer-by quickly sized up the situation and directed his mount to squat squarely in the breach until more permanent arrangements could be made.

Even a fork-lift truck has been known to diversify in an emergency. For days a raging bull terrorized a village in Hungary until a fork-lift-truck driver, trundling home one evening, cornered the brute and deftly imprisoned it between the stout steel prongs of his vehicle.

Human ingenuity is so boundless that no situation need be regarded as hopeless, no catastrophe as final, if you have the gift to recognize the hidden potential in a thumb, an elephant, a fork-lift truck and a myriad of other, but more mundane, articles.

Airing When airing a bed, a stone or aluminium hot water bottle, standing on its end, will spread the heat better than a rubber one.

Artificial flowers Limp fabric flowers can be revived over steam and plastic flowers can be washed in soapy water.
Fading petals of plastic flowers can be revived with nail varnish.

Beads Re-stringing beads is easier if you fasten the new thread to the old one with glue.
Run a new thread for beads over soap to strengthen it and to make it easier to handle.
Line up beads in corrugated cardboard to keep them in order for threading.
Strengthen the knots between individual beads with nail varnish.

Bees To remove a bee which has flown into the house, hold up a long-stemmed flower to it. When the bee settles on the flower, carry it outside.

Bird cage Use an empty salt tin with a pourer to store bird seed so that you can fill the holder quickly.
Protect the base of a bird cage with aluminium foil.

Birthday cards When selecting one birthday card, buy several of a design which appeals to you and build up a stock of cards to avoid last minute panics for other birthdays.

Books When sending a book through the post, protect the cover corners by folding a square of card twice into triangles and slipping one of these over each corner.
Repair the torn spines of books with self-adhesive carpet binding.

Boots Stuff the legs of your boots with a thick folded newspaper or magazine, when you take them off, to keep them in good shape.

Bottles To unscrew a tight bottle top, grip it with a piece of coarse sandpaper and twist it. Nutcrackers will unscrew small bottle tops.
A few rubber bands slipped at intervals around a bottle will provide a safe grip.
Keep bottles upright in your shopping basket with a bicycle clip pushed through the side of the basket.

Candles A milk bottle top will secure a candle in a loose-fitting holder.
To get the maximum spread of light from a candle, stand it on a mirror or in front of a mirror.

Cars Tip your car seats forward when parking in hot weather to shield them from the heat of the sun.
Attach an identifying pennant to your car aerial when parking in an extensive car park, to guide you back to it quickly.

Do not automatically part-exchange your car with a dealer when buying your new car from him. You could do better with a private sale.

Cats   A cardboard carton with a mattress of crumpled newspaper and old woollens will keep your cat comfortable and free from draughts. Polystyrene food trays and tile off-cuts can be used to line the box for extra warmth.

A hinged cat-flap made in an outer door or wall will allow pets to come and go at will.

Protect your furniture by providing a kitten with a log of wood and train him to use it for sharpening his claws.

Chinaware   China will travel safely by post if you wrap it in layers of wet newspaper which, when dry, will form a protective shell around the article.

Small china ornaments can be encased for safety, when sent by post, in a hollow made in a loaf of bread.

Christmas shopping   Look out for remainders of Christmas stock being sold cheaply in January and February which may be worth buying for the following Christmas.

Clocks   Stand your bedside clock on an enamel plate if the alarm fails to waken you.

Clothes brush   Burn off the bristles of an old clothes brush and replace them with foam rubber sponge.

Coat-hangers   When covering coat-hangers, put a little fresh lavender inside.

Make one strong coat-hanger from two flimsy wire hangers by blanket-stitching them together.

A shoulder pad sewn to each end of a coat-hanger will keep clothes in good shape.

Rubber bands wound around the ends of a hanger will prevent blouses and dresses from slipping off.

Dancing pumps   With a pencil dipped in household bleach, you can print your child's initials on the outside of his or her pumps.

Distilled water   The melted frost from a refrigerator or freezer is nearly as pure as distilled water.

Dogs   Rinse muddy paws one at a time in a jam jar.

Dampen your brush when brushing a long-haired dog to make untangling easier.

Drawing pins   Push drawing pins in at an angle or over a small piece of card so that they wil be easy to remove. A teaspoon helps to remove firmly embedded pins.

Drying-up   Rinse crockery in clear water after washing and leave it to drain dry.

Glasses upturned on a tissue will dry clear and need no wiping.

Cutlery benefits from being dried with a cloth straight away.

Ear-rings   Odd ear-rings can be used as brooches, sewn to a lapel or neckline, or they can be attached to a chain necklet.

Keep ear-rings clipped to a wire coat-hanger so that they can be easily found.

Envelopes   When confronted by a pile of envelopes and stamps, use a dampened sponge to moisten about a dozen flaps and a strip of stamps at a time.

Examinations   Tape-record a recitation of points which have to be memorized to fix them in your mind.

Fan belt   If your fan belt breaks, tightly tied nylon stockings will prove a temporary substitute.

Felt-tipped pens   Re-charge a felt-tipped pen by standing it in a bottle of ink for several days.

Glue   Vinegar will thin glue which has set in the pot and will soften hardened glue on woodwork.

Replace the pin in a tube of glue with a cup-hook for easy withdrawal.

Goggles   Store goggles in a strong plastic bag to protect them from scratches which could limit your vision.

Goldfish   Cover the top of a goldfish bowl with a hair-net to prevent frisky fish leaping out or pawing pussies getting in.

A strong plastic carrier bag, suspended from the dashboard, is ideal for transporting fish by car.

Heels   Drawing pins stuck into shoe heels will prolong their life.

Hot water bottles   Put a few drops of glycerine into a new hot water bottle to make it last longer.

When filling hot water bottles, use a metal funnel to avoid any hot splashes.

A child's old jumper is just the right size for a hot water bottle cover. Remove the sleeves, sew up the waistline and sleeve holes and thread elastic around the neck.

Keeping a lavender sachet inside a hot water bottle cover is a good idea.

In very hot weather, keep cool with a hot water bottle filled with cold water or ice cubes.

Jumble sales   Zip fasteners, gold and silver trimmings, belts, buttons and even fur collars can be acquired very cheaply from selected garments at jumble sales.

Kettles   A piece of loofah or a round pebble will prevent scale forming inside a kettle.

Keyholes   Paint your front door keyhole with luminous paint to make it easy to find in the dark.

Key-rings   It is unwise to put your own name and address on a key-ring. Arrange to use a friend's and let her use yours.

Dabs of different coloured nail varnish on your keys will help you to pick out the one you want quickly.

Laces   Dip frayed shoe laces in nail varnish and twist the tip to a point.

Stitch small buttons to the ends of children's laces to prevent them from being pulled out.

Replace the laces in children's plimsolls with elastic so that they will slip on and off easily.

Maps   Reinforce a paper map with Sellotape stuck along both sides of the creases.

Matches   Keep matches out of your children's reach by fitting the box on a picture hook near the cooker.

Put used matches into an empty scouring powder or table salt carton and use it as a firelighter when full.

Name tapes   Economize when ordering name tapes for two children by having two sets of initials printed, one before the surname and one after it, so that the inappropriate initials can be turned under, out of sight, when sewing them on the clothes.

Your address or telephone number is a useful addition when marking clothes.

Self-adhesive carpet binding can be cut up to make easily-fixed name labels.

On socks, sew name tapes along the welt so that no restriction is caused.

Notice board   Paint the inside of a kitchen cupboard with blackboard paint for reminders and messages.

Nylon   Vary the appearance of your baby's nylon dress by putting different coloured petticoats beneath it.

Similarly, put two or three nylon scarves together for an attractive effect.

Parcels   Protect the address on a parcel by covering it with Sellotape or candlegrease.

Wrapping up a parcel will be easier if you dampen the edge of the brown paper and if you use wet string it will tighten around the parcel as it dries.

Paste   A discarded roll-on deodorant bottle makes an ideal paste dispenser.

Pencil stand   A glass or plastic flower holder, as used inside vases, is useful for holding pens and pencils.

Pension book   To facilitate its quick return if it should be lost, keep a pension or allowance book in a stamped, self-addressed envelope.

Photograph albums   Fasten a plastic bag to the back inside cover of an album to hold the negatives of the prints displayed.

Photograph frames   Plastic cling-film, wrapped tightly over a photograph and its backing, makes a good substitute for glass when this has been broken.

Postage stamps   When enclosing a stamp for return postage, moisten only the centre of the stamp, rather than a corner, so that adhesive remains on the edges.

Pottery   Many kitchen items will produce an original finish on unfired pottery. Experiment with mincing-machine cutters, a parsley chopper, bottle tops, rubber suede brushes and a butter-roll maker.

Pram handle   A bicycle bell fixed to a pram handle is useful on busy pavements.

Punctures   To make bicycle punctures easily visible, put a little French chalk inside each inner tube so that, when a puncture occurs, a white spot will show where the hole is.

Razor blades   Get a good grip on a razor blade by fixing press-studs into the holes.

Rubbing a razor blade back and forth inside a glass tumbler will sharpen the blade.

Refrigerator   To test whether a refrigerator door is properly adjusted, close the door over a sheet of paper. If you can withdraw the paper, the seal is not satisfactory.

Removals   Pack and seal clothes in large plastic bags for easy handling when moving house.

Note the contents and the room destination in the new house on each packing case as you fill it.

Rings   Keep a large safety-pin fixed to the inside of your handbag to hold your rings safely if you take them off to wash your hands.

Rubber gloves   Avoid fingernail holes in rubber gloves by reinforcing the tips by sticking Elastoplast inside.

When your hands become hot and sticky inside rubber gloves hold them under the cold water tap until cool when the gloves will slip off easily. Rinse gloves thoroughly after use and sprinkle them inside with talcum powder ready for their next use.

The fingers of rubber gloves often roll up when they are taken off. A quick way to open out the fingers is to grasp the glove at the wrist with air inside and shake it sharply.

The fingers from discarded rubber gloves can be slipped over the ends of a coat-hanger to make it slip-proof.

A supply of rubber bands of various sizes can be obtained by cutting up an old rubber glove.

Sacks   Sack-filling is easier if you hold a strip of wood across one side of the opening.

Satchels   Extend the strap of a satchel with a loop of elastic which can be slipped over the buckle when the satchel is overloaded.

Scooters   Repair split scooter seats with waterproof iron-on carpet binding.

Scribbling paper   Save Christmas and other greetings cards to use for scribbling paper and shopping lists.

Self-defence   If you have to be out alone in the dark, carry an aerosol can of fly or hair spray, or a tub of pepper, as protection against thugs. Or better still take evening classes in judo.

Sellotape   Keep a button on a roll of Sellotape so that you can find the end quickly.

Sequins glued to the toes of evening shoes will enliven a not-so-new pair.

Shoes   Make new leather shoes water-resistant by rubbing linseed oil into the soles and welts.

Make slippery new soles safe by rubbing them on rough concrete or with sandpaper.

Paint over white stitching on new shoes with clear nail varnish to keep it clean.

Relieve tightness in new shoes by leaving a slice of raw potato in them overnight.

Help your child to recognize a right or left shoe easily by marking the inside soles with R or L, as appropriate.

Zip fasteners on boots are easier to handle if a short length of shoe-lace is fastened to the tab.

A shoe-horn fitted to a length of wood or a ruler can be helpful to those with stiff joints.

Stuff wet shoes with newspaper, replacing it at intervals until the shoes are dry.

When a heel lining is worn and uncomfortable, stick a large adhesive plaster over it.

Pad the toes of pointed shoes with cotton wool or tissue paper to keep them in good shape.

Keep the straps of sling-back shoes in place by fixing a strip of self-adhesive foam rubber strip inside the strap.

Shopping   Keep a pad for shopping requirements pinned up in the kitchen so that you can jot down your needs as they occur to you.

A leather luggage label fixed permanently to your shopping bag will keep shopping lists easily visible.

Keep a strong plastic bag in your shopping basket to isolate wet or smelly items.

To be able to take advantage of any bargains seen unexpectedly, keep a list in your handbag of all the family's sizes and of measurements for curtains and wallpaper.

Shoulder bags   Prevent shoulder bags from slipping off your shoulder by sticking self-adhesive foam rubber strip or self-sticking nylon looped tape to the strap and beneath collars.

Skirts   To keep warm when wearing a short jacket over a long dress, wear a warm skirt as well which can be slipped off quickly at your destination.

Slippers   Strengthen the heels of soft slippers by sticking on heel grips.

Snow   Fasten plastic bags over children's gloves, with a rubber band around the wrist, to keep their hands dry and warm when playing in the snow.

Soap   To keep soap dry when it is standing on a handbasin or sink, press a metal bottle top into one side to lift it clear of moisture.

Put odd scraps of soap into a nylon net bag or the foot of a nylon stocking and hang it under the hot tap when running a bath.

Dissolve scraps of soap and press them into a small container so that they will form another tablet when set.

Soap scraps can also be put into a foam rubber case and used as a sponge, or thin slivers of soap can be softened and pressed on a new tablet.

Spiders   Smear the plug-hole of the bath with soap to deter spiders.

Stocking ladders   Keep an old lipstick case filled with soap in your handbag to stop ladders. Nail polish and hair lacquer are also effective for this purpose.

Suction hooks   Smear egg-white on a suction hook before fixing it to strengthen its hold.

Suitcases   Keep the locks of suitcases and hold-alls untarnished by smearing them with olive oil or Vaseline or by painting them with clear nail varnish.

Old suitcase handles are useful fastened to the cord of heavy parcels.

Suspenders   When you lose a suspender knob, a small coin or peppermint will substitute well.

Swimming   Socks are easier to put on after swimming if the feet are sprinkled with talcum powder. It helps to remove sand painlessly too.

Table tennis balls   You can remove a dent from a table tennis ball by repeatedly dipping it in hot water until it regains its shape.

Telephone   Use an egg-timer to keep an eye on the time when making telephone calls.

Cork tiles look attractive glued to the wall surrounding a telephone. Pin messages and useful telephone numbers to them.

A list of the current charges per minute for the different times of the day, fastened to the cradle of the telephone, may confine non-urgent calls to the cheaper times.

A strong rubber band holding the instrument to the cradle of a telephone helps to prevent toddlers from playing with it.

Tobacco   A slice of raw potato placed in the tin will keep tobacco moist.

Toothpaste   When too much toothpaste has been squeezed out of a tube, it can be sucked back into the tube by squeezing the sides gently.

Squeeze out toothpaste economically through the tube cap by making a small hole in it with a hot skewer.

Fold over a toothpaste tube evenly from the bottom as you use it to save wastage from uneven squeezing.

Trays   Fix self-adhesive plastic foam strip beneath trays to protect polished surfaces.

Tumblers   When two tumblers are stuck together, pour cold water into the top tumbler and stand the bottom one in warm water to release them.

Tweezers   Slit a match at one end to make emergency tweezers.

Typewriter   If your paper support is difficult to pull out, fasten a metal tag or a plastic bag tie to it.

Typewriter keys can be cleaned with an old toothbrush and a cocktail stick will clean individual letters.

Umbrellas   Smear the frame and hinges of an umbrella with Vaseline to prevent rusting.

Shoe laces will make replacement loops for umbrellas and a plastic thimble will substitute for a lost ferrule.

To make an umbrella holder on a shopping basket, fasten two small key rings to the handle, one at each end, and clip two larger rings through them to hold the umbrella.

Wasps   An empty jar coated with jam and half-filled with water will attract and trap wasps both inside the house and in the garden.

Watches   Stand a tumbler over a bedside watch to drown the sound of its ticking if it disturbs you.

Remove scratches from a watch glass by rubbing them with cigarette ash.

Wrap your watch in Sellotape before going on the beach, to keep it free from particles of sand.

Water shortage   In times of water shortage, put several plastic bottles filled with water inside the lavatory cistern to reduce the amount of water used when it is flushed.

Direct all waste water from your washing machine to the garden by extending the machine's emptying hose.

Wellingtons   Help your children to identify their own wellingtons by marking them inside the top edge with an individual design in coloured ink or with coloured adhesive tape. If the marks are made on the inner leg side, a younger child will also be able to distinguish between the left and the right boot.

Slip a plastic bag over your socks before putting on wellingtons to keep your feet warm.

Train your children to peg their wellingtons together when they take them off and thus save time in finding them.

A hairdryer will dry soggy wellingtons quickly.

Cut insoles for wellingtons from remnants of polystyrene tiles or food trays.

Windows   To prevent accidents caused by children opening sash windows, restrict the opening by inserting a screw at each side so that the window can only be opened a few inches. Casement windows can be made safe by screwing bars across them.

Zip fasteners   Stiff zips will run freely if a lead pencil is rubbed up and down them.

Gardening
Hosepipes to humus

My initiation into the mysteries of horticulture followed a move to a new house when we were faced with a remnant corner of a meadow where no beast had ever grazed nor plough penetrated since time began.

My husband shrugged and, with sharpened spade, he resolutely cut through the undergrowth to ground level. Then he marked out the stubbly land and cut out turves in rows. At the end of each row, he drove a stake into the ground.

It was then the job of the rest of the family to break each piece of turf over the top of the stake and thus create a pile of fine soil for shovelling back.

The residual roots of twitch grass, ground elder and plantain left in our hands became fuel for a bonfire which smouldered for weeks. The ashes from that bonfire, with useful potash content, my husband claimed, were in due course scattered over our embryo garden.

He must take after his great-aunt Elizabeth who also had her own way in horticulture. She not only talked caressingly to ailing aspidistras and murmured apology whenever she dragged a lettuce out of the soil, but her sweet peas earned her village-wide renown for their colour, size and perfume.

Yet her nurturing was of the simplest. In her rickety lean-to greenhouse, she mixed soot from the kitchen chimney with the contents of her chamber-pot. After maturing and dilution, the mixture was fed to her sweet pea plants as soon as they came into flower.

'The books will tell you about hormone treatment, trace elements and root pruning but the rest you'll rarely find in print,' a gardening friend maintains.

So I attempt to fill this gap in the following pages, adding to the wooden stake and the elixir for sweet peas some of the many other good ideas I have chanced upon over the garden fence.

Ants   A mixture of one teaspoonful of borax and one tablespoonful of sweetened condensed milk will attract and kill ants. Leave some on flat stones near the nest or in an emptied milk tin in other judicious positions.

Cloves and paraffin will discourage ants from entering the house.

Autumn leaves   Stand leafy branches in a solution of one part of glycerine to two parts of water for several days, then seal the ends with candlegrease or sealing wax, to preserve them.

Leaves can also be preserved by placing them flat, with the ends sealed, between sheets of newspaper beneath a carpet for several weeks.

A lump of modelling clay or fine wire-netting crumpled to fit a vase will hold branches firmly in place.

Birds   Thread milk bottle tops on string and place them around the garden to discourage birds. A child's plastic windmill is another useful deterrent.

An old hair-net will protect a young plant and net curtains will protect fruit bushes from the birds. Tie paper bags over pears in their final ripening stage.

Cactus   Small cactus plants look attractive in pieces from a doll's tea set.

Cats   Keep cats off the seed beds by scattering pepper or by hanging up rags soaked in creosote.

Cold frame   A cold frame can be made quickly and simply from a box with a sheet of glass placed on top of it. Old picture frames can be utilized too.

A clothes horse lends itself to easy adaptation to a cold frame. Cover it with strong polythene sheeting and stand it directly on the ground or on a base of bricks or timber.

Compost   Shredded newspaper soaked in water can be added to the compost heap.

Cuttings   Wrap cuttings in damp moss and seal them in plastic bags until they have taken root, when they can be planted out.

Stick rose and similar cuttings into a raw potato before planting them, to retain moisture.

Daffodils will last longer if a little sugar is added to the water in the vase.

When daffodil and other spring bulbs have finished flowering, fold over the leaves and slip a rubber band around them to keep them tidy until they have turned brown. They can also be knotted in small bunches.

Fir cones Miniature fir trees can be grown from the seeds shaken out of fir cones. They will, of course, grow to full height in due course if planted outside later.

Fish pond If a fish pond freezes, the ice should not be sharply broken but slowly melted with hot water or with a hot poker.

A ball left floating on top of a garden pond will ensure that an aeration hole can be easily made when the water freezes.

Flowers To arrange short-stemmed flowers in a tall vase, half fill it with pebbles, marbles or coloured mica pellets. The stems could be extended with plastic drinking straws as an alternative.

Wrap wilting newly-bought flowers in newspapers and stand them in deep water overnight before arranging them in a vase.

Put a plastic doyley over a shallow bowl and stick flowers through it. It can be weighted down with a stone, if necessary.

A plastic scouring pad can also be used as a flower holder.

Sellotape will bind broken stems. It can also be criss-crossed over a vase to support stems.

Mirrors can be used to enhance a flower display. Place a bowl of flowers in front of a mirror or, for a centrepiece, stand the bowl on a round or oval mirror.

A flower can be preserved in a sealed bottle of surgical spirit.

Small jars pressed into a bowl of sand can be filled with short-stemmed flowers to make a dinner party centre-piece with ferns, moss and low-lying leafy twigs anchored on the sand.

Pressed flowers can be used to make calendars or birthday cards or they can be fixed beneath glass table tops or finger plates. Flatten the flowers and place them between sheets of blotting paper underneath several heavy books for a few weeks.

Foot-scraper Nail an upturned scrubbing brush near the garden door so that mud and grass clippings can be brushed off boots and shoes. Two brushes facing each other, several inches apart, are even more effective.

A scraper can also be made by folding a sheet of strong wire-netting to a suitable size.

Fruit-picking Wear gloves when you pick fruit to protect your hands from lurking wasps.

Gardening tools Nail lengths of wood or wire-netting to the wooden uprights of a garage or shed and store your implements behind them.

Garden seat A simple garden seat can be made by building two columns of bricks to support a plank.

Grass growing between paving stones can be killed with salt or boiling water.

Hands   Before gardening, dig your nails into a bar of soap and give your hands a coating too to protect them from the soil.

Hanging baskets   Line the bottom of a hanging basket with polythene to help retain moisture in the basket.

To make watering easy, suspend a hanging basket on a pulley.

An old bird-cage or a chip-pan basket will convert readily to a hanging basket.

A coconut shell with holes burnt in the sides to hold chains can be planted with bulbs or hanging plants.

Heather will stay fresh longer if the stems are pressed into a large potato and placed in the bottom of a bowl. Alternatively, fill a bowl with soil and arrange the heather in this.

Holly   When holly is short of berries, make some from red modelling wax.

Holly bushes can be propagated by planting berries in a box of sand. They may take more than one year to germinate, so leave them undisturbed and protected from birds in a corner of the garden.

Indoor garden   Make an indoor garden from a deep bowl filled with soil. Arrange pebbles, moss and a handbag mirror for a pool in it. Use small glass tubes to hold flowers so that they can be changed regularly without disturbing the garden.

Kneeling mat   An old hot water bottle stuffed with sawdust or shredded nylons makes an ideal gardening mat.

Leaves   Fix wire-netting over drains and gutterings to prevent their blockage by falling leaves.

Wash the leaves of indoor plants occasionally with lukewarm water, using a wad of cotton wool.

Marrows can be trained to grow up a stout pole or a fence, thus taking up less garden space and keeping the marrows clean and dry.

Mint   Plant mint in a bottomless bucket to restrict its spread.

Peas   Before sowing peas or sweet peas, dip them in paraffin to stop mice or birds eating them.

Pineapple   Slice off the top of a pineapple and plant it in a mixture of sand and peat. It will take root if you keep it in a sunny position and water it regularly.

Planting out   Use an old ballpoint pen as a dibber for planting out and an apple corer or a potato peeler to transfer seedlings.

Sharpen the end of the handle of a hoe or rake so that it will also serve as a dibber, to save time and effort bending over long rows.

Used tea bags will help to retain moisture around young plants.

Potatoes Large seed potatoes can be cut in half lengthways before planting, but make sure that each portion is sprouting well.

Pot plants Use large twigs and knitting needles as supports for indoor climbing plants.

A pipe-cleaner coloured green makes an inconspicuous plant tie.

Use a polythene squirter bottle to water house plants.

Plants standing on well-soaked foam rubber will absorb the moisture slowly.

When leaving plants for a period, water them well, then seal them inside a plastic bag, arranging sticks to keep the plastic off the plants.

Another method for supplying water slowly in one's absence is to stand the plants in water in the sink on a foam rubber mat with a bowl of water on the draining board. Trail lengths of string or wool between the bowl and the pots to convey moisture when the sink water is exhausted.

Revive old plant pots with red tile polish or white emulsion paint, placing them over a milk bottle for easy painting.

A cycle clip slipped between trellis slats will hold a pot plant.

A bathroom tumbler-holder painted black, an upholstery spring, an oil lantern or a bird-cage will all adapt to holding pot plants.

When flowers are expensive, enliven a non-flowering pot plant with a few plastic flowers. It may also enliven conversation with incredulous guests.

Plant stands can be made from an umbrella stand, a tiered saucepan holder, a cart wheel or a shallow drawer fitted with legs.

An expanding curtain wire or a strip of wood fixed across the front of a window sill will safeguard pot plants.

Large plastic lids from tins of food can be used as pot plant stands to protect surfaces from moisture.

Raspberries To beat the birds, pick your raspberries as soon as they turn pink and before they appeal to the birds. They will ripen quickly indoors.

Rhubarb To force rhubarb, cover it with an upturned bucket or cardboard box, making holes to admit the light.

Roses Throw tea leaves and coffee grounds on to the rose bed.

A little sugar added to the water will make cut roses last longer.

Rubbish burner Stick several metal stakes into the ground and attach a cone of strong wire-netting to the stakes to make a small incinerator.

Set an old bottomless bucket upside down on top of burning rubbish. It will act as a chimney and speed the burning.

Seeds   Newspaper placed at the bottom of a seed tray helps to retain moisture.

Left-over pieces of polystyrene tiles can be used to line a seed tray to retain warmth and speed germination.

Sow seeds in egg cartons, egg-shells, match-boxes and small plastic food tubs for easy transfer to the garden after germination.

Use a match-stick or cocktail stick, dipped in water, to pick up individual seeds and ensure even distribution.

A salt cellar is handy for scattering small seeds evenly and a salt tin with a pourer can be used for larger seeds.

An old suit-case is useful in the garden to hold seed boxes early in the year, when the lid can be closed if frost is forecast.

Save lollipop sticks and staple empty seed packets to them to mark boxes or rows.

Collect your own seeds by tying the foot of a nylon stocking over the desired pod until it ripens when the seeds will be captured safely.

Large plastic fruit juice or cleaning liquid containers can be cut in half vertically to make oblong seed boxes.

Shears   After cleaning and oiling them, store garden shears in an old oily sock.

Shrubs   When propagating shrubs by layering, use a kitchen grater to roughen the underside of the branch being layered to help it root more quickly.

Slugs   Soot and wood ash mixed together will deter slugs.

Stakes   Fasten two large empty tins lengthways to the shed wall about one metre apart to hold stakes horizontally, when not in use. Remove the bottom from one of the tins and push the stakes in from this side.

A nylon stocking makes a good tie for staking, its width will protect and stabilize a young tree. Plastic bags and old curtains or sheets cut into strips are also useful for ties.

The ribs of an old umbrella frame can be used as plant supports. Or you can stick the handle of an opened umbrella frame in the soil and sow climbing annuals around it. A bare Christmas tree can also be used in this way.

Strawberries   Place egg-box cups under strawberries to protect them as they ripen.

Sweet peas   Line the bottom of a sweet pea trench with newspapers to retain moisture.

Sow sweet pea seeds around the base of a long tube of wire netting, fixed upright in the soil as a support for the growing plants.

Make a slit with a razor blade in sweet pea seeds to hasten germination.

Tomatoes Protect outdoor tomatoes at night with a roll of newspaper, stapling it to the supporting stick.

To direct water and nutriment to the roots of tomato plants, sink a plant pot into the soil near the base of the plant, angled at the roots, and pour liquids into this.

Green tomatoes will ripen if you put them in a paper bag in a warm dark place. The addition of an apple will speed this process.

Tulips A little starch in the water will prevent tulips from drooping.

Alternatively, before arranging them in a vase, plunge them up to their necks in water for an hour, piercing a small hole just below the flower head with a pin.

Vacuum cleaner dust is acceptable on the compost heap.

Vases Partly fill vases with sand to keep them steady and to hold flower stems in position.

Vegetables Carrots, purple kale and other vegetables can look quite at home in the flower border.

As a change from flowers, make a long-lasting colourful table arrangement with root vegetables, small marrows, peppers and similar items combined with dried flowers and grasses.

Water butts Filter rain water from roof gutterings through a nylon stocking tied over the end of the fall-pipe to keep the water in the butt clean.

Weeds Use a potato peeler to dig out lawn weeds.

Keep the wheelbarrow or a dustbin lid nearby when weeding and throw the weeds into it so that they can be easily transferred to the compost heap.

An applicator for weed-killer can be made by pushing a sponge into a length of pipe and filling the pipe with weed-killer. It can then be applied to individual weeds without damaging neighbouring plants.

Wheelbarrow Fix a box or wire basket to the wheelbarrow to hold seeds and small gardening oddments.

Window-boxes A layer of moss or gravel placed on top of the soil in a window-box will prevent mud splashes when it rains.

Line a window-box with roofing felt, pierced for drainage, to make it last longer.

Woollens Instead of throwing away old woollens, chop them up into small pieces and add them to the compost heap or dig them into the soil.

Health and Self

Loneliness to loofahs

I have never been given to sallying forth before the streets were properly aired, so I have not been able to verify the claim that it is trampling in the dew that makes the milkmaid fair. In fact, I feel sure that this pastime can lead only to a red nose, webbed feet and body-wide aches and pains.

So, if you choose to follow in the milkmaid's footsteps in search of beauty, I can offer no aid for the resultant colour of your nose, no solution to the duck effect on your feet and no more than a vague promise that a couple of aspirins will relieve, temporarily, your rheumatic twinges.

I can, however, suggest an almost guaranteed relief from the neck-ache which surely must follow from bearing one of those wooden yokes, supporting two swinging pails of milk, across your shoulders.

Open and flatten a large newspaper, then fold it lengthways repeatedly until it becomes a compact strip, eight to ten centimetres wide. Wind this around your aching neck and secure it with a scarf. Many a sufferer has enjoyed her first full night's sleep for weeks after following these simple instructions.

Milkmaids no doubt suffer like the rest of us from those curious excrescences which may or may not yield to medication, incantation or the repeated application of diverse substances, most of which have to be begged, borrowed or stolen to guarantee success.

One ancient remedy, suitable for milkmaids as it happens, is to rub a wart with dandelion juice at break of day for ten mornings in a row. For lie-abeds like me this presents problems, so I would prefer to sell mine to the man in the moon, who has been known to buy them.

Sir Thomas Browne also favoured the moon. His seventeenth-century remedy was to rub his hands in its glow, then 'commit any maculated part [the wart] to the touch of the dead'. As an alternative, his contemporary, Nicolas Culpeper, in *The English Physician Enlarged* recommended an ointment made of mugwort mixed with hog's grease and daisies.

More recently, in defiance of vinegar-soaked ivy leaves, furry skins of broad beans, rough pebbles and plastic lemons, a wart on my husband's hand remained in the best of health. It was of vast proportions when he began to paint the garage walls with emulsion. A fortnight later, when he succeeded in ridding himself of the last remnants of the emulsion paint, the excrescence had disappeared too.

Baby powder If a baby-powder tin dispenses powder too liberally, seal some of the holes with Sellotape.

Make your own scented talcum powder by sprinkling unwanted perfume on to baby powder.

Baby-sitters Make a tape-recording of yourself singing a lullaby or reading a bed-time story for your baby-sitter to play to your child if you cannot be there at bed-time.

Give an older child time to adapt to an unknown baby-sitter before you leave.

Make an information board for baby-sitters giving your whereabouts and telephone number, your doctor's telephone number, a friend's or a relative's telephone number, the position of the medicine chest and any necessary feeding instructions.

Bandages Sterilize strips of worn out sheets or pillow-cases by boiling them and keep them in a plastic bag to use as bandages.

When discarding rubber gloves, save the sound fingers for covering finger bandages.

Bathing Spread a large towel in the bath to prevent both the elderly and the young from slipping.

A foam rubber dish-mop will help an elderly or arthritic person to wash and bath.

A pair of tights makes an emergency bath cap.

Beds Prevent sitting-up invalids from slipping down the bed by fixing a bolster across the middle of the bed. Wrapped in sheeting, it can be firmly secured with the ends tucked under the mattress.

Raising the foot of the bed a few inches gives overnight relief to tired legs and feet.

Bed cradle Many articles will convert quickly to a bed cradle. You can, for instance, use a cardboard box with the base and one side cut away, a small folding picnic stool or a fireguard.

Bed-jackets Turn up the ends of a stole to make a bed-jacket with pockets for handkerchiefs, spectacles and similar items.

Bedside table A book-case or a trolley placed beside the bed will give an invalid plenty of space for books, flowers and drinks.

A three-tier cake-stand on a bedside table will keep small odds and ends within easy reach, and a tray can be converted into a useful bed-tray by screwing four short legs to it.

An ironing board makes a useful bedside table for meals and pastimes.

A wide runner of cretonne or plastic material, fitted with pockets, will keep toys and books handy for the invalid.

Chilblains Relieve the itching of unbroken chilblains by rubbing in a mixture of equal parts of glycerine and surgical spirit.

Chin-lines Sleep without a pillow to preserve a good chin-line.

Corns Protect a sore corn with a finger stall cut from a soft glove.

Cots To prevent a baby from slipping down too far in his cot, place a heavy pillow between the top sheet and the blanket at the foot of the cot.

If your child has discovered that he can shake his cot around the room, anchor it firmly by securing it to two strong hooks fixed to the skirting board.

Crutches Knit or crochet a string cap to fit over the end of crutches to prevent falls in wet weather.

Depression Pre-menstrual depression can be relieved by reducing your intake of liquids during the ten days prior to the start of your period.

Drinks At meal-times, serve tea in bed to an invalid in a vacuum flask to save extra journeys upstairs and to allow him to drink it hot when he is ready for it.

A screwtop jar, with a hole in the lid for a drinking straw, substitutes well for a drinking cup.

Ear-plugs To avoid any difficulty in removing a wax earplug, divide the plug into two and wrap each piece in a small gauze square. This will make a close-fitting and easily removable plug.

Elastoplast Nail varnish remover or eau-de-Cologne will remove marks made on the skin by Elastoplast.

Elbow pads Very small cushions filled with plastic foam pieces make a welcome present for invalids to use as elbow pads to prevent soreness.

Enlarged pores Bathe the enlarged pores on the nose and chin with warm water and borax, finishing with a splashing of cold water.

Eyes Castor oil helps to float out insects or dust trapped in the eye.

Soothe tired eyes with cold tea or with a solution of half a teaspoonful of salt to a tumbler of warm, freshly-boiled water.

Exercise your eyes daily to strengthen the eye muscles. Look by turns to left, to right, up and down, at near and far-away objects and roll your eyes a few times. Do these simple exercises about twice a day.

Smooth away lines around the eyes with a smearing of egg-white.

Eyelashes can be darkened with regular applications of castor oil.

Feeding When your child is learning to feed himself, put his food into a shallow wide-necked jar which will make it easier for him to load his spoon.

The use of finger-puppets may encourage a reluctant eater to accept food.

Feet Soak tired feet in warm water with a tablespoonful of iodine, Epsom salts or paraffin added.

A hot soak followed by a cold water splash also revives tired legs.

Harden your feet before a long walk by rubbing in witch-hazel, eau-de-Cologne or surgical spirit for some days beforehand.

Rub sock heels with soap to prevent blisters on long walks. If you forget to do this a small piece of sheep's wool found on the journey and placed in your shoe will also do the trick.

Remove hard skin from the soles of the feet by rubbing it with sandpaper or with a large soda crystal.

Regular massage with olive oil after a bath will prevent calluses forming on the feet.

Finger-nails It is often easier to cut a baby's finger-nails when he is asleep.

Protect a split finger-nail with waterproof adhesive plaster cut to the shape of the nail.

First steps Fix sticking plaster to the toes of your baby's shoes when he is starting to walk, to give him a firmer grip on linoleum and carpets.

Food dishes Invalids who have difficulty in feeding themselves will find babies' food dishes, with their deep sides, a great help.

Hair If your toddler worries about having his hair washed, the fun of wearing an underwater mask for protection may make him more co-operative.

When soap gets into a child's eye, breathe gently into the eye to soothe it.

Borax will soften water for hair-washing and vinegar in the last rinsing water will act as a setting agent for normal hair.

Dry hair will benefit from one drop of olive oil in the rinsing water.

Darken greying hair with regular applications of sage tea, made by steeping one teaspoonful of tea with one teaspoonful of sage in a large mug of boiling water. Let it cool before applying to the hair.

Use strips of foam rubber to roll up your hair after washing it at night. They are more comfortable to wear for sleeping than hard curlers.

A thick rubber band put around your head will set a wave across the back of your hair as it dries after washing.

A hair slide will grip securely if you stick a piece of adhesive plaster to its underside.

Spots of hair spray on spectacles or mirrors can be cleared with nail-varnish remover.

Hands Equal parts of glycerine and water make an economical hand lotion to keep by the sink for regular use to protect your hands. Lemon juice could be added to whiten the hands.

Clean very soiled hands with a mixture of olive oil and sugar or salt.

Mustard rubbed into the hands will remove cooking smells.

Run cold water over your hands, after washing them in warm water, to close the pores.

Headache A drink of fresh lemon juice with a pinch of bicarbonate of soda will often relieve a headache. Sucking barley sugar or mints or applying a rubber glove packed with ice cubes can also help.

Hospital Help a child to cope with the end of visiting time by giving him a surprise parcel as you leave.

Illnesses Keep a permanent record of the dates of your child's illnesses and immunizations. They are easily forgotten but often needed later on in life.

Legs Keep your toddler's legs extra warm in a push-chair by slipping them into a large bag made of old blanketing.

Lipstick Dissolve left-over stubs of lipstick in a cup placed in a saucepan of boiling water. Pour the liquid back into a case to make a new lipstick.

A lipstick can be clipped on to a handbag pocket if you can find a pocket clip from an old fountain pen to fit the lipstick holder.

Loneliness If you are lonely and living on your own, do not have things like newspapers and milk delivered to the house, but make yourself go out each morning to the shops to buy them and to speak to people. Try joining an evening class on a subject which interests you to reduce loneliness and develop your potential.

Loofahs Back-scrubbing is easier if a long loop of tape is attached to each end of a loofah.

Make-up tray A deep tray will convert into a make-up tray with thin strips of wood fitted to divide it into compartments. Paint it or cover it with self-adhesive plastic material.

Medicine Cover the dosage on a medicine bottle label with Sellotape to prevent it from being obscured with use.

Always keep all medicines out of reach of children.

To catch the drips on medicine bottles, twist a pipe-cleaner around the neck of the bottle or make a collar from lint or plastic foam.

Blotting paper on the shelves of a medicine chest will soak up any drippings.

Sucking an ice cube will numb the tongue and thus make it easier to take unpleasant medicine.

A reluctant medicine-taker will sometimes use a straw happily. This method also protects the teeth from staining when taking iron.

Use a kitchen timer or an alarm clock to remind you when medicine is due to be taken.

If you have difficulty in remembering whether you have taken certain pills, count out each morning the total number to be taken during that day and put them in a pill box or a special container.

Metal irritation If metal clasps on watch straps, jewellery or bra fastenings irritate your skin, stick ear-ring pads over them or paint them with nail varnish.

Nail varnish Thickening nail varnish can be thinned with nail varnish remover.

Nappies Use large tissues as nappy-liners.

Use nappies as hot water bottle covers for the cot and have a well-aired nappy always ready for use.

New baby If a new baby brings a special gift for her brother or sister when she arrives, it helps the toddler to bear with the situation.

Newspapers Large newspapers are easier to cope with if fastened through the centre pages with safety-pins. This practice is especially useful to invalids reading newspapers in bed.

Pillow A pillow warmed by a hot water bottle helps to soothe a restless baby or an invalid to sleep.

Poisons Write the antidote on the label of any bottle of dangerous liquid kept in the house.

Pony tail Prevent tangles in a pony tail by putting it in a nylon stocking at bed-time.

Poultice Use an egg-poacher to heat a poultice, placing it on a strip of lint in the egg tray.

Powder box Cover a full box of powder with cotton wool or a tissue before putting on the lid, to keep the contents under control when opening it.

Prams When a pram is left standing in the garden, croquet-type hoops of strong wire fixed through the wheels on both sides of the pram are a good safety precaution with an energetic baby.

The rustle of a newspaper near a baby's feet in a pram will keep him amused as he kicks it.

Pregnancy Avoid stretch marks after the birth of your baby by rubbing olive oil regularly into your skin. A triangle of fabric inserted into both sides of the front waistline of your old jeans will take them a long way into pregnancy with you. Make tucks at the top of the triangle and release them as required.

Refreshing ideas   In hot weather, run cold water over your wrists for a few minutes as a cooling measure.

A cup of hot tea is more cooling than a cold drink.

Skin freshener will be more bracing in hot weather if you store it in the fridge.

At times of excessive perspiration, drink an occasional glass of salted water to compensate for the loss of salt by the body.

Restricted outlook   Position one or two large mirrors in a bedroom so that a long-term invalid can see activity in the street outside.

Rheumatic knee   Keep the ribbed top of old bed-socks to wear over a rheumatic knee to give it warmth.

Scalds   Cold tea relieves the pain of minor scalds.

Scent   Prevent evaporation by sealing the neck of an opened scent bottle with nail varnish.

Scurf on a baby's head can be removed by rubbing it gently with wet cotton wool dipped in borax, before washing the hair.

Shampoo   Use a salt cellar or a sprinkler vinegar bottle to dispense shampoo and setting lotion evenly.

Skin   Add olive oil or baby oil to bath water as a skin softener, but be careful to wash away all traces of the oil from the bath afterwards to avoid slipperiness.

Sleeplessness   The noise of a vacuum cleaner will often soothe a restless baby to sleep.

Smelling salts   A small bottle filled with cotton wool soaked in ammonia substitutes well for smelling salts.

Splinters   Draw a splinter out of a finger with a piece of wet soap, or a paste of soap and sugar, bound over the splinter and left overnight. Elastoplast will also draw out a splinter.

Pressing over the area surrounding a splinter or thorn with the hole of a key helps to bring it to the surface.

Never use a pin to draw out splinters – a sterilized needle, however, is a safe alternative.

Staircase   Make a handrail on the staircase wall to help the elderly and the very young.

Those who live alone and feel unsteady on the stairs may find it easier to crawl down backwards.

It is a good idea to keep a shoulder bag for carrying things upstairs so that both hands are left free.

Styes   To soothe a stye, fill a vacuum flask with hot water and hold your eye over the steam.

Sunburn relief   Cool sunburnt skin by sponging it with cold tea or gently rubbing it with a cut tomato.

Suntan   Baby oil makes an economical suntan lotion but it is not advisable to use this on a fair skin as it contains no sun-screening agent.

Tablets   To overcome a difficulty in swallowing tablets, crush the tablet between two spoons and mix the powder to a paste with sugar and butter or with fruit juice.

A tablet may be accepted more readily by a child if it is inserted in a glacé cherry or a soft sweet.

Placing a pill under the tongue and drinking water helps you to swallow it.

Teeth   Clean tobacco-stained teeth with bicarbonate of soda or salt.

Toes   Cut toe-nails straight across the top to prevent ingrowing toe-nails and rub Vaseline or petroleum jelly into them after bathing to prevent hardening.

Travelling   A light diet for a few days before a long journey, with no fatty foods on the day itself, will help to prevent travel sickness. Sucking glucose sweets on the actual journey also helps.

Tray cloths   For bedroom trays, blotting paper or thin foam rubber makes a useful tray cloth which will absorb spills and steady the crockery.

Vomiting   The odour can be removed from carpets and upholstery by sponging them with a strong vinegar and suds solution, changing the water several times.

Warts   Castor oil rubbed regularly on a wart will clear it from the skin.

Youthful look   Older persons will find that a touch of white at the neckline flatters the face.

Zip fasteners   If stiff limbs make back fasteners difficult to handle, sew a hook to a piece of tape and clip the hook into the hole of the zip when dressing. Pull on the tape to open or close the zip.

Leisure and Pleasure

Balloons to beaches

To be fully comprehensive, the contents of this chapter should range from hints for those who feel urged to scale Everest to techniques for those who simply want to fold a full-size newspaper from a deck-chair on the beach during the storm conditions known as August holiday weather.

But the subject is so vast that I have had to turn my back on the esoteric and hazardous in order to concentrate on the everyday gentle pursuits of pleasure, such as setting out on holiday with the family or planning a birthday party for twenty ten-year-olds.

There must, nevertheless, be many omissions and, although for these I offer no excuse, in some circumstances I can tender reasonable explanation.

For example, seeking to check some hints on painting in oils, I visited a friend in her garden-shed studio. As I entered, a blaze of colour on the end wall attracted my attention.

'I love that one,' I exclaimed, 'it's most exciting!'

'That,' my friend said icily, 'happens to be the place where I clean off my brushes.'

After that gaffe, I had no courage to pursue my questions and this accounts for one of the areas of omission in this chapter.

I notice that I pass on a hint for protecting birds from cats but nowhere have I come across a hint for protecting cats from birds. This is lamentable, because my own cat suffers the tortures of the damned each spring when the swallows return from North Africa to dive-bomb her in her own back garden.

I have found no easy way of protecting the cat in these circumstances. You just have to snatch up the terrified furry bundle and, braving the dive-bombing, make straight for the safety of the sitting-room.

Here you disappoint the birds and, as it were, kill two with one stone. For all pastimes, leisure pursuits and holidays so often begin as a tiny thought from the depths of an armchair.

Balloons   Blowing up balloons is easier if you rub them first between your palms and stretch them.

At parties, use balloons as place-markers, printing each child's name with nail varnish, shoe whitener, poster paint or a felt-tipped pen.

Paint 'Happy Birthday' or 'Merry Christmas' on balloons, as appropriate.

If you rub a balloon on a woollen surface for a few moments and then put it on the ceiling, it will stick to it for a long time.

Turn a red balloon into a Santa Claus face, with cotton wool for hair and beard and coloured paper for the nose, eyes and mouth.

Similarly, you can make a snowman from two white balloons, black paper and a black marker pen.

Beach holidays   For beach cricket, dye a few old tennis balls bright red, making them easier to find on the sands.

Pack a small puncture outfit for repairs to inflatable toys.

Birds   Bird-feeding provides interest for young children and the housebound. In addition to putting crumbs on the window-sill and garden path, hang bacon rinds, bones and fat to a metal coat-hanger and suspend it from a tree where the antics of the blue-tits can be watched.

Instead of chopping up waste food, put it out whole and watch the birds pecking at it for much longer.

To protect the birds from cats, make a feeding tray to hang from the branch of a tree.

At nesting time, feathers and short lengths of wool placed on bushes will quickly attract the birds.

Make a bird-bath with a dustbin lid set in a rockery.

Birthday parties   An out-of-doors treasure hunt relieves the pressure on indoor facilities for a party. For the very young, scatter peas or beans in the garden, on the paths and on window-sills and see who can collect the most in a given time.

Children who can read can be given an individual list of items to find, such as a red pencil, a blue marble, a 1978 penny and so on.

Older children will enjoy a real hunt in the park or on the beach. Give them a long list of objects to find and questions to answer on the colour, number or date of items in the area, such as the colour of the seats or the time of high tide.

Distribute presents or prizes at a party with a lucky dip or by attaching strings to the presents for each guest to pull.

For a toddler's party, supply a variety of miniature foods, such as sliced bridge rolls, jellies made in egg cups, small cheese biscuits and miniature iced cakes. Fill a doll's teapot with orange juice and leave the rest to the children. They will soon organize themselves into 'families'

113

and the party food will be consumed over a long series of make-believe visits and meal-times.

Bottle tops Coloured bottle tops make attractive knobs for homemade fancy boxes or holders for miniature flower arrangements.

Camera As a substitute for a tripod, stand two chairs back to back and rest the camera on a piece of board set across them.

Car journeys To save space when travelling with a baby, put nappies, towels and similar items in cushion covers and use them in place of your usual car cushions.

Cartons Empty plastic tubs and cardboard food cartons have many uses in children's imaginative play. Decorated with coloured stickers and given an elastic strap, they also make party hats. They can also be covered with decorated paper to make gift boxes.

Chalks Keep chalks whole and children's hands clean by binding chalks with Sellotape, unwinding it as the chalk wears down.

Christmas cards Avoid toppling cards and dusting problems by pinning up Christmas cards, as they arrive, on lengths of crêpe paper, tinsel or ribbon hung from the ceiling or looped across alcoves.

Make large shapes of stars, bells, holly, Christmas trees or Santa Claus and stick the cards on them.

A clothes horse can be bound with strips of crêpe paper to make a base for cards.

Make vertical chains of cards joined together with Sellotape.

Hang cards on a Christmas tree or on a branch from the garden which has been painted white and covered with glitter.

A quick and simple way to display cards is to slip the backs of the cards between the books on a bookshelf.

Christmas decorations Make angels, fairies and stars from pipe-cleaners, silver and gold paper or milk bottle tops.

Stick holly into large potatoes to keep it fresh over Christmas. A hanging ball of holly, based on a potato, looks most attractive.

Twist a metal coat-hanger into a circle and decorate it with holly and baubles. A potato threaded on it will act as a base for the stems of holly and mistletoe.

Save red caps from bottles and stick a small piece of cupressus in them to make miniature Christmas trees.

Egg carton sections can be whitened and gilded and used to hold small pieces of fir, candles, baubles and so on.

White polystyrene packing can be broken up into attractive shapes and used as a base for table decorations.

Fir cones will open out if left in a warm place. Paint them with white emulsion paint, adding glitter while they are wet, or touches of gold and silver paint when dry.

To make your own paper chains, fold lengths of crêpe paper concertina-wise and draw a Christmas tree or bell on the top fold. Following this outline, cut through the folded paper but leave one or two sections of the folds uncut so that the strip will open out into a chain of trees or bells.

A sparkle can be given to fir cones by soaking them in a strong solution of salted water for about half an hour. They will have a frosted appearance when dry.

Pot plants make useful bases for Christmas decorations. Stick holly, fir and red candles into them carefully without disturbing the roots.

Christmas stockings To make a Christmas stocking, cut out a stocking shape from a large plastic bag and stitch around the edges with embroidery silk or red binding.

Christmas trees Stand a Christmas tree in a bucket of soil and keep it well watered to ensure that the needles do not drop too quickly.

Lay thin strands of cotton wool along the branches and sprinkle glitter dust over them.

Cut out stars, bells and angels from aluminium foil and hang them on the tree by a strand of cotton.

Make miniature crackers from crêpe paper, small parcels from match-boxes in Christmas wrappings and colourful rosettes from Cellophane sweet wrappers to hang upon the tree.

Christmas wrapping paper Save the best parts of wrapping papers and iron them smooth to keep for another year.

Clay modelling Use the framework of a discarded lampshade as armature for clay modelling.

Coal garden An interesting table decoration can be made by setting a few lumps of bright coal on two tablespoonfuls of salt in a glass dish. Mix together two tablespoonfuls of ammonia, two tablespoonfuls of powdered laundry blue, two tablespoonfuls of red or green ink or colouring, two tablespoonfuls of water and pour the mixture around the coal. Every other day, add one tablespoonful of salt dissolved in one tablespoonful of water. In time, colourful crystals will form and cover the coal.

Coconut man Slice off the top of a coconut and fill it with soil. Paint a face on one side and sow grass seeds in the soil. In a short while the face will be topped with hair.

Cotton reel holder A cotton reel holder can be easily made by a youngster, to give as a present. Take a piece of wood of suitable size and hammer in nails at intervals, tilting them slightly upwards. The board can be painted or papered or just left plain to hang behind a cupboard door.

Dice   When dice cannot be found, a substitute can be made by cutting out a piece of card with six sides of equal length. Number each side from one to six, push a match-stick through the middle and twist it for a number.

Dolls   Wide lace and nylon edging on discarded lingerie can easily be made into dolls' dresses by small girls.

In a doll's house, use velvet ribbon for stair carpet and a crumpled red milk bottle top for a realistic fire.

Match-boxes can be turned into many items of dolls' furniture, including miniature beds for which you can make pipe-cleaner babies.

Dough play   Children will enjoy modelling with dough made from flour, water and salt. It can be coloured with custard powder, cocoa or cochineal and will last for several playtimes if stored in a plastic bag.

Drinks   Polythene squirter bottles, well rinsed out, are ideal for holding drinks for train and car journeys and for picnics.

Easter gifts   Give the family surprise eggs on Easter morning. Put a small gift or some sweets inside an empty egg-cup and cover it with an upturned empty egg-shell, so that on sight it looks like an ordinary boiled egg. Serve them for breakfast!

Egg-shaped containers for Easter gifts can be made by cutting up an egg-carton and joining two sections together, covering them with gold or silver foil and ribbon.

Fishing net   Use the top of a nylon stocking to make a fishing net.

Fruit punnets   Square fruit punnets decorated with fancy paper and ribbons make attractive party hats.

Gift tags   Cut up Christmas and birthday cards with pinking shears to make gift tags with ribbons attached. These are good selling lines at bazaars.

Holidays   Trunks can be rejuvenated with a coat of paint and shabby linings can be replaced with self-adhesive plastic material or wallpaper.

Paste a list of contents on the inside of your suitcases for checking items as you pack at both the start and the end of your holiday.

Bulging letter-boxes are significant to a thief, so remember to cancel the newspapers and ask a neighbour to remove any mail or circulars projecting from the box.

Good neighbourliness also pays dividends when you get the 'I've left the gas on' feeling but know that someone has checked after your departure.

Be prepared for a rainy day and pack pencils, papers, cards and board games, as space allows.

New shoes can ruin a holiday so break them in well beforehand.

When you are staying with friends, hostesses will appreciate your thoughtfulness if you go out for a whole day by yourselves occasionally.

Sew tapes inside children's clothing showing their holiday address or buy them each a toy watch and replace the clock face with the holiday address.

Ensure a relaxed start to your holiday by making out a schedule for last-minute jobs and crossing them off when completed.

Jigsaw puzzles Mark the reverse side of each jigsaw piece with a different coloured felt-tipped pen so that it can be quickly identified as belonging to a certain puzzle.

Make throw-away jigsaw puzzles for children by cutting up discarded greetings cards and calendar pictures into suitably sized pieces.

Macaroni Necklaces and bracelets can be made with macaroni pieces which can be dyed with food colouring.

Magazines Set children a picture chase with a pile of old magazines, seeing who can find most pictures of a given subject.

A simple party game can be made from magazine cover-girl pictures by cutting the pictures in half and giving one half-picture a number and the other half a letter. Pin them up in any order around the room and hand out pencils and paper, giving a prize for the first correct list of matching faces.

Modelling A plastic ice cube tray makes a useful receptacle for all the small bits and pieces used in making models.

Hair grips are useful for holding gummed edges together until they have set.

Paints Save chubby cosmetic jars for children's painting sessions. Mix water colours in them and stand them in a cake tin to avoid spills. Or mix colours straight into the divisions of a patty tin.

Small screwtop jars with a hole punched in the top for the paint brush are also helpful.

Cut foam rubber into animal or toy shapes, dip them into paint and print the shapes.

Save old shirts and pyjama jackets to cover up children's clothes for painting sessions.

Paper flowers When joining the stems of paper flowers to the main branch, reinforce the joints with Sellotape before binding them with paper.

Pebbles collected on the beach can be varnished with nail lacquer and glued around tin lids to make ash-trays or pot plant stands.

Photography As a reminder of the type of film needed for your camera, stick the gummed seal from the film on to your camera.

When photographing a baby, hand him a length of Sellotape. As he tries to pull it off his fingers, his attention will be distracted from the camera.

Display holiday snapshots under glass on a coffee table or pasted to a plain lampshade.

Fix a shower-head into the tray for better agitation when washing prints.

Fasten clothes pegs to the bottom of a drying negative strip to prevent it twisting.

To ease the removal of photographic paper from its box in the dark room, place a piece of cardboard with a tape tab beneath the bottom sheet.

Mask a torch with suitable red paper or paint so that it can be used in the dark room.

Picnics Convert a disused pram basket to a picnic basket by fitting it with vacuum flasks and food boxes.

Fix castors on two legs of a picnic chair and use it to wheel food and equipment to the picnic site.

Place markers Use plastic bibs as place markers and presents for a baby's party.

Write children's names on a triangle of paper and fix it to a segment of orange with a cocktail stick to resemble a boat.

Place mats Use coloured blotting paper as place mats at a children's party.

Plastic toys A nail file will smooth down a rough edge on a plastic toy.

Playbox Keep a box of odds and ends, keys, bottle tops, old watches, locks and so on to provide interest for a small child.

Pomander When making a pomander, use a knitting needle first to pierce the holes so that the cloves can be pressed in without breaking.

Quoits Turn a kitchen stool upside down to make a game of quoits with bottling or cardboard rings.

Rag books Stiffen a limp rag book with a strong starch solution.

Records   A picture of the recording star pasted on to the centre or sleeve of a record single makes it easily identifiable.

Sand-pit   Make a sand-pit from an old lorry tyre, painted white, or from a card table with the legs shortened and the sides boarded.

Self-catering holidays   If you buy one extra item of food every week, you can gradually and painlessly build up a stock of food for your holiday.

Swings   Glue a foam rubber stair pad to a swing seat to make it safer.

Tennis racquets   Stick thin towelling on a worn and sticky handle of a tennis racquet to give it a cool grip.

Travelling   Luggage identification will be no problem if you paint a band of bright colour on each piece.

Seal the tops of cosmetic bottles with Sellotape to prevent leakages in suitcases.

To travel light for brief holidays, save very small plastic bottles and tubes to make yourself a miniature set of cosmetic requirements.

Dampen a sponge and pack it in a plastic bag for cleaning sticky fingers when travelling.

Word-building and number-finding from car registration numbers will relieve boredom among the family on a car journey.

Visitors' book   Start a visitors' book as soon as you set up home – it will provide enjoyment in the years to come.

Water pistols   Empty polythene washing-up bottles provide good fun for the children as water pistols in the garden or at the seaside.

Index